D0114476

Diversity and Direction in Psychoanalytic Technique

Diversity and Direction
in Psychoanalytic Technique

Fred Pine

Yale University Press   New Haven & London

Designed by Rebecca Gibb. Set in Minion type by Keystone Typesetting, Inc., Orwigsburg,Pennsylvania. Printed in the United States of America by Vail-Ballou Press, Binghamton, New York.

Library of Congress Cataloging-in-Publication Data
Pine, Fred, 1931–
Diversity and direction in psychoanalytic technique / Fred Pine.
p.   cm.
Includes bibliographical references and index.
ISBN 0-300-07344-5 (hardcover : alk. paper)
1. Psychoanalysis.   I. Title.
RC504.P558   1997
616.89'17—dc21
97-37013 CIP

A catalogue record for this book is available from the British Library.

The paper in this book meets the guidelines for permanence and durability of the Committee on Production Guidelines for Book Longevity of the Council on Library Resources.

10   9   8   7   6   5   4   3   2   1

To Louis and Mollie
and to Harold and Beverly
lovingly

Contents

Introduction

The chapters in this book grow from my experiences as a psycho-analyst, a psychotherapist, and a developmental theorist, each set of experiences influenced by recent developments in psychoanalytic theories of mind and technique. Each chapter addresses an issue in contemporary psychoanalysis; together they represent widely varying entry points into that domain. This approach in fact reflects my first theme: diversity.

Given the wide array of psychoanalytic theories that currently command respect among experienced clinicians and the proliferation of technical approaches to the patient, a thoughtful analyst has to struggle to find a way through the diversity. I have chosen to do so through inclusiveness and breadth. I do not believe that every new idea regarding mind or technique deserves to be preserved; many have already dropped out of sight and others should do so. But overall I see psychoanalysis today as a productively expanding field, with new ideas most often filling gaps in earlier ones rather than replacing those earlier conceptions; the changes are additive, not substitutive. In spite of the frequent criticisms of psychoanalysis and psychoanalysts in the past for their supposed rigidity, my sense is that psychoanalysis today, in its very diversity, is the most comprehensive and open-minded theory of mind (and of psychological treatment) available. Approaches that say "this and only this is the way" represent the new rigidity.

This overall point of view is consistent with the approach taken in my previous book, *Drive, Ego, Object, and Self: A Synthesis for Clinical Work* (1990), in which I also attempted to view the diverse theories of mind additively. While theoretical and technical diversity are at the center of attention in both books, in the present volume the emphasis shifts somewhat in the direction of technique. It is thus part of a continued line of development for me personally and responsive to developments in the field of psychoanalysis as a whole. For it is clear that the main focus of psychoanalytic writings tends to run in waves, and that the current wave concerns technique.

In contrast to my previous book, this one is selective rather than systematic. I write on topics about which I feel I have something to say. I offer no general theory of technique; rather, I believe technique is in the small details, and I try to focus on some specific differentiations in the domains of clinical theory, clinical understanding, and clinical intervention. This reflects my second theme: direction. By this term I mean specific, differentiated clinical directions within the diversity.

The discussions that follow are directed to an audience of psychoanalysts. Given my professional history, that is the primary reference group I find myself addressing as I think and write. But I have learned that the individuals who are most receptive to the profusion of new thoughts in psychoanalysis are often students, beginning therapists, and even experienced therapists who are aware of the competing nature of ideas in the field, who do not yet have committed experience-based stances in relation to these ideas, and who are seeking to position themselves clinically and theoretically within the field.

For me, the psychoanalytic, the psychotherapeutic, and the developmental are closely blended. My psychoanalytic thinking continues to be developmentally oriented, as described in my book *Developmental Theory and Clinical Process* (1985). In the years since the publication of that book, the psychoanalytic and the psychotherapeutic approaches have also come closer together for me. While I will not hazard a differential definition, I nonetheless often feel that I have a clear sense of a difference between them when I make (or refrain from making) one or another kind of intervention. But their coming together is based on my experience that most treatments include both psychoanalysis and psychotherapy in varying degrees and at varying times. I often think of my clinical work in terms of doing as much psychoanalysis as possible in a context where I do as much psychotherapy as necessary—the latter being precisely what makes it possible to pursue the former. At other times, or with other patients, the psychotherapeutic portion seems a full partner of equal status and value in the enterprise. I do not quite think of these latter treatments as psychoanalysis, but I cannot think of them as *not* psychoanalysis, since psychoanalysis inevitably enters into the work so significantly for an analyst. All these perspectives are part of my clinical day. I offer here a mix of the psychoanalytic, the psychotherapeutic, and the developmental as aspects of them have come together for me in recent years.

A final introductory word. This book is essentially a personal statement, and I have chosen to write in a personal style—often in the first person. It expresses the things that I have learned through my clinical experience over the years. They color my analytic style; they underlie my listening during sessions. I have found that much of the detail of my formulations and, even more, their overall spirit, have been useful to my students. I hope the same will be true for readers of this book.

Part I Diversity in Psychoanalysis

The chapters in this section are intended to develop a view of the diversity central to current psychoanalytic thought. Chapter 1 spells out the underpinnings of the evolution of diversity in technique. This discussion makes it clear that there is no room for orthodoxy in technique, from whichever theory it is derived. The psychoanalytic process is rich but problematic; though we know a great deal, we are often working in the dark in the individual instance. The review of issues underlying the evolution of diversity presented here is neither historical nor theoretical. Rather, it is built around the subtle and not so subtle challenges to technique that have arisen in the minds of clinicians as they try to do their psychoanalytic work. The review is unsystematic and roves widely, but its central thrust is clear: to argue against settling into any single comfortable view of technique.

One of the challenges to any orthodoxy of technique comes from the proliferation of theories, of diverse models of mind. Chapter 2 deals with these issues. Here, since I have written extensively on this matter in earlier publications, I attempt a more systematic statement, to provide a basis for incorporating multiple models of mind within one overarching psychoanalytic view. At the same time I recognize that this broadens our thinking about technique—in terms of both the issues of mind addressed and the ways of addressing them.

These chapters are intended to provide the baseline for Part II of the book, which discusses direction within the current diversity.

1 Diversity in Technique: Six Discussions of the Backdrop

Diversity in technique is a fact of contemporary clinical practice in psychoanalysis. While it parallels the current diversity in psychoanalytic theory (described in the next chapter), both its sources and its expressions are probably far more extensive, stemming not only from theoretical innovations but also from highly individualized features of the analyst and the analytic process. It is my aim here to explore some of the intellectual backdrop to this diversity, simultaneously underscoring the considerations that present challenges to any orthodoxy regarding technique.

It is both a source and a reflection of the diversity that no two psychoanalysts hear a session in exactly the same way or work in the same way with whatever it is they do hear. The psychoanalytic process is too complex, analysands are too varied, and analysts are too different from one another in their personal and professional histories to permit any simple replicability in the work. Complexity and hence diversity are the human condition, and this is no doubt true for teachers, cooks, surgeons, or scientists as well as for analysts and analyses.

In this chapter, I work primarily with the evolution of technique in the historical line that traces directly to Freud—the line with which I am most familiar. I note briefly the reach of that technique to become an orthodoxy and then move into the underpinnings of the explosion of diversity that characterizes the current psychoanalytic scene. I strongly doubt that there ever was any such orthodoxy; variation is guaranteed by the considerations regarding individuality I just noted. In addition, the respect always given to considerations of tact and timing as well as the less frequently mentioned fact of variation in tone (of voice) always made for immense variability in technique, probably expressive of the analyst's reading of the clinical realities of the moment and of his or her personal modes of functioning.

I believe that my own way of working clinically with patients in analysis would be easily recognizable in its so-called classical character. I work with the couch and the free-association initial instruction. I am guided by the trio of neutrality, abstinence, and relative anonymity. I listen and I interpret. I do recognize that today there are many departures from free association, from neutrality, from abstinence, and from anonymity, but I generally regard each of those positions as a baseline to which I return, even while recognizing the clinical realities that periodically dictate departures from it. Apart from whatever else arises in the analytic material, I am also oriented to two things in particular at the outset: first, the analysand's reaction to the couch, to the analytic situation, and to me, especially with regard to matters that may lead to flight or may otherwise interfere with the analytic process getting started. Second, and closely intertwined with the first, I attempt to give the process over to the analysand, enabling him or her, through whatever individualized interventions seem appropriate, to enter sufficiently into his or her own thoughts and reactions so that I can listen quietly. Of course this takes time and is not always possible.

I have been profoundly influenced by the several views of mind extant in contemporary psychoanalysis, and I therefore "hear" the material in many different ways. I have also been influenced by recent developments in the theory of technique, such as attention to the here-and-now, to enactments, to countertransference in its positive (informative) form, to the two-person psychology of the analytic exchange, and thence to questions regarding self-disclosure. I feel that my own movement toward diversity in technique has grown mainly through listening to my patients (especially those who taught me by pointing out forcefully the mismatch between who they were and how I worked), through reading in the psychoanalytic literature, and through experimenting with what I gathered from my reading and from my observations and the demands of my patients—experimenting, that is, within the limits that my fairly clear-cut standards would allow.

Recently (Pine, 1996) I had occasion to discuss the work of three British analysts, each of whom reported session process notes essentially without comment. They were members of the three British groups: a Kleinian, a Freudian, and an Independent. There were distinct differences among them, at least with respect to the material presented at our conference on that day. One interpreted early, focusing almost completely on the "between us" in the here-and-now; a second was much slower to interpret and then began with the here-and-now and moved into connections to the past; the third was again fairly active, but divided interventions nonsequentially among the transference, the outside present, and the past. Nonetheless, it seemed to me that they could have been reporting on the way I work with, say, the first three patients in my practice on a particular Monday morning, depending on the particular patient. Variation sits comfortably within what has come to be a reasonably stable way of working.

A Bit of History
In 1919, in "Lines of Advance in Psychoanalytic Therapy," Freud envisioned a time when an effort would be made to bring psychoanalysis to larger numbers of people. For the poor, he suggested, it may be even harder than for the rich to give up their neuroses because life

itself offers the former so few attractions. "Often perhaps we may only be able to achieve anything by combining mental assistance with material support" (p. 167). Freud then offered this oft-quoted sentence: "It is very probable, too, that the large scale application of our therapy will compel us to alloy the pure gold of analysis with the copper of direct suggestion" (pp. 167–168). Here Freud was discussing the use of "suggestion" as a form of treatment, but his concern with it went well beyond treatment.

Suggestion was of particular interest to Freud with regard to his relations with his contemporary medical community and his inner relation to the idea of psychoanalysis as science. For him, suggestion raised the specter of the nonrational aspects of undue personal influence, undercutting any claims of psychoanalysis to be a science. Changes in personal functioning based on discovery and insight were to him more consistent with the idea of science; knowledge (insight) was the foundation of psychoanalysis as it was the foundation of science. I am not preparing the way here for an argument favoring the role of "direct suggestion." My point, rather, is that the "pure gold" metaphor had the side effect of encouraging a reach for a certain kind of purity. As I have already implied, I believe such "purity" to be unattainable in anything so complex as an analysis, and indeed undesirable. The "golden" quality of psychoanalysis is probably best represented today by its evolution toward both diversity and directedness—that is, a more differentiated view of clinical phenomena and of the specific techniques tied to them.

In the 1940s through the 1960s, the era of the dominance of ego psychology (perhaps especially in the United States), the purity of technique came to be associated with an emphasis on interpretation in the context of neutrality, abstinence, and relative anonymity. Neutrality refers to the analyst's not taking an opinion-based stand on outcomes but maintaining an analyzing stance with equal interest in exploring all aspects of the patient's mental life, conceptualized at the time as id, ego, and superego (and thus not favoring the patient's achievement of drive expression or adaptation or morally correct behavior, but simply analyzing). Abstinence refers to the analyst's not participating in the patient's sexual or aggressive wishes, fantasies, and enticements but instead, and again, maintaining an analyzing stance. And relative anonymity refers to the analyst's keeping his or her personal self and life as much as possible in the background.

This trio of guideposts, plus the use of the couch and of free association, were intended to give the patient space to explore and reveal his or her mental life without intrusion. But the trio can readily be understood as well as forms of control on the analyst. The analytic situation is one of unequal power, of secrecy, and of temptation. The prescription for neutrality offers some control over the analyst's opinions and personal influence; for abstinence, some control over the living out of sexual and aggressive urges and fantasies; and for relative anonymity, some control over the danger of narcissistic self-centrality on the part of the analyst. These prescriptions, plus the patient's use of the couch and of free association, were intended to give the analyst the privacy necessary to maintain the primary analytic focus: evenly suspended attention open to all meanings and eventuating in analyzing.

As we know, in their extreme form these practices led to the image and perhaps too often the actuality of the aloof analyst, though they need not have done so. None of the three basic guideposts is inconsistent with a general atmosphere of warmth and concern. Perhaps because of Freud's (1912) "surgical" image, or perhaps because of the need to move away from the violations by the first generation of analysts, the pendulum seems to have swung too far at that time in the direction of aloofness. Kurt Eissler's 1953 paper, "The Effect of the Structure of the Ego on Psychoanalytic Technique," marked the extreme of an aspect of that reaction in the United States. By referring to variations in technique as "parameters" that must eventually be interpreted away, he defined and defended what came to be thought of in some circles as "classical" psychoanalytic technique—the centrality of interpretation to the exclusion of other modes of intervention. And, in the psychoanalytic view of the mind at that time, interpretation was understood within the terms of the structural theory—the conflictual relations among drives, defenses, and conscience. But other threads were also present and made for a more balanced picture.

One of these other threads was presented in Samuel Lipton's (1977) paper on Freud's technique as revealed in his analysis of the Rat Man. Lipton's conclusion was that the rather austere definition of so-called classical technique was a view that grew primarily in the United States and *after* Freud's death. Lipton argues that for Freud, who offered the Rat Man herring when he arrived hungry one day, personal actions like this were "outside of technique," were carried out within the bounds of ordinary courteous human relationships, and entered the analysis only if they became part of the meaning-seeking work of the free-association and interpretation process. A recent article by Couch (1995) on his analysis with Anna Freud makes it clear that, years after her father's death, she was still working in his manner.

A second modifying thread is evident in Leo Stone's (1961) well-known monograph on the psychoanalytic situation. He sees a background of warmth and connectedness as entirely consistent with psychoanalytic clinical work. This relates to a point I made earlier—that tact and timing were always recognized as having a significant place in analytic work. This is a way of saying that, whatever the formal dictates of a theory of technique, there has to be room for personal judgment and for subtle but significant variations in the realities of individual clinical situations.

The reference to tact and timing immediately calls to mind another point: that there is often a gap between public teaching and private action. Given the demands of life within the subculture of psychoanalytic institutes, supervision and seminars may convey far more of the received wisdom regarding technique than the particular supervisor or teacher actually uses with a particular analytic patient. Clinical reality demands flexibility—disciplined flexibility, but flexibility nonetheless. But often one's position among peers is seen to be dependent on subscribing to shared belief systems. This will often influence the public activity of teaching, while for some a more flexible approach will characterize their clinical work.

It is of interest in this respect that, at a recent "classics revisited" panel at the meetings of the American Psychoanalytic Association, Eissler's (1953) paper was roundly criticized for promoting a rigidity that slowed down the evolution of technique. The published version (Panel, 1994) is far more temperate in its criticism than was the actual discussion.

Simultaneous with this reach for an orthodoxy in technique in certain circles, countervailing trends of more individualized kinds existed. I am by no means against the central thrust of this "classical" or "orthodox" technique. As I have noted, I believe there is much to be said for neutrality, abstinence, relative anonymity, the use of the couch, free association, and interpretation, and they remain the core of my own work. No absolute orthodoxy can survive, however, in a method as inherently variation-prone as psychoanalysis, and both a softening and an expansion eventually took place. That led to the current state of the practice.

In the remainder of this chapter, I review a variety of considerations that both underlie and reflect the current diversity in psychoanalytic technique, as well as my own receptivity to such diversity. The review can be seen as an exploration of the basic anatomy of our work and also as an argument *for* diversity; as such it may not be needed, since diversity is already a characteristic of clinical work in the field. But I believe the points I make are of interest in themselves and have substantive value. While diversity is characteristic of the field as a whole, it is unlikely to be characteristic of the work of all individuals. There is some tendency to develop a mentality that says "this is the way to do it," and it often seems that new proposals regarding technique readily become elevated into orthodoxies. This may be because of the anxieties of uncertainty in all psychoanalytic work and the concomitant wish for certainty. Political loyalties and other personal motives are also undoubtedly factors. It is my position not that every individual practitioner should incorporate the full range of technical approaches but that all should ideally be aware of the intellectual issues and problems that confront us in developing our clinical stance.

With that in mind, I proceed to discussions of six aspects of the backdrop of the move toward diversity in technique.

Uncertainty of Outcome

About thirty years ago, in a talk that I heard but have been unable to trace, Robert Waelder developed the idea that advances in psychoanalytic theory were spurred by the fact that interpretation and insight, based on whatever theory we were then working with, could not be counted on reliably to produce therapeutic change. Waelder's examples of these developments in theory (stimulated by failures to achieve change through then-available insight) had to do with masochism, unconscious guilt, and the repetition compulsion—all efforts to account for difficulties in bringing about change. He could well have listed Freud's concepts of "adhesion of libido" (1916–17) and "resistance of the id" (1926)—hardly explanatory but still reflecting awareness of the slow pace of change—to illustrate the same point. Despite awareness of resistance, the slow refinement of understanding, and long periods of working through during an analysis, maintaining a residue of doubt about our theoretical understanding of the basic workings of mind seemed the wisely cautious stance to adopt.

Waelder's point about developments in the theory of mind applies equally to developments in the theory of technique. If we had a thoroughly effective treatment, there would have been no need to develop it further. Granted the sources of changes in technique in new theories, differing patient requirements, and the creativity of individual practitioners, change is ultimately driven by the wish to improve the power of our clinical practice. A fully formed, once-and-for-all theory of mind and of technique might make for stagnation in the mental life of psychoanalysts, but the effectiveness of clinical practice would then be reasonably guaranteed: the patient would arrive, the treatment would be applied, and the patient would leave better than when he or she came. Clearly there is no expectation that this process will occur in working with the human mind and personality.

We are probably fated to continue witnessing the evolution of theory and technique. The alternatives, especially when working with analysands who are recalcitrant to change, are to give up, subtly assuming that it is the patient who is somehow wrong, or to insistently follow an unrelenting treatment course, assuming or hoping that it will all work out in the end. While each of these prospective courses of action may make sense at times and may continue to do so whatever our advances in understanding, they may also give way to more knowledgeable alternative approaches within the general frame of psychoanalysis or outside of it.

Insight and Structural Change

Robert Wallerstein (1985, 1994) has reported on the results of a long-term study of process and outcome in psychotherapy and psychoanalysis, the Menninger Psychotherapy Research Project. I draw primarily from his summary report (1994), which I have had the opportunity to discuss (Pine, 1994a). In brief, groups of patients were seen in psychoanalysis, in analytically oriented insight therapy, or in supportive psychotherapy. Outcomes were evaluated over the long term, and some process variables were studied. The study is subject to a number of criticisms, and Wallerstein and his co-workers are not unaware of them. I do not report on the findings as proof of anything but rather to approach some of the issues Wallerstein raises, which serve the aims of my discussion here.

Among psychoanalysts, psychoanalysis has been conceived of as the one psychological treatment capable of bringing about "structural change"—that is, change in the basic relations among drives, defense and adaptation, and conscience (or id, ego, and superego). This is achieved through the work of interpretation matched by insight. Probably the core contribution of the Menninger study (Wallerstein has embarked on a second study that probes some of the issues of the first) is the apparent cracking of any cemented link between insight and structural change. Actually the findings create two cracks: (1) expressive-insight therapies, including psychoanalysis, include significant supportive features, and (2) structural change seems to follow from support as well as from insight. What Wallerstein calls a fully "classical" analysis—a "therapeutic activity . . . steadfastly focused upon the interpretive uncovering of intrapsychic meaning"—did not take place with any of these patients. He does explicitly recognize that the patients were probably more ill than (or at least different from) the usual outpatient population, but he nonetheless takes his findings seriously, as I believe we all must, until and unless shown otherwise. That is, all treatments include support, which is in turn tied to significant change. (I do not discuss here either Wallerstein's sophisticated and highly differentiated analysis of "support" [1985] or his ongoing attempt at sophisticated and differentiated analysis of "structural change" [1994]).

Wallerstein referred in his paper to the "conventional wisdom" that sees structural change as being tied to insight and not to supportive work. In using that phrase, he is implicitly questioning the linkage, as his data have forced him to do. I assert that that very belief (that is, the "conventional wisdom") is itself only an *assertion*, without an evidential base—and a self-serving assertion at that. That is, we analysts have laid claim to ownership of the route to structural change. The Menninger study data force us to question that assumption, or at least to bring evidence to bear for the traditional view. It is a constructive challenge.

It is not my main aim here to argue specifically for the importance of supportive interventions. This information came my way only accidentally when I was asked to be a discussant of Wallerstein's paper. But it provides another way to illustrate what it is I do want to argue: that many places to which we turn, as in my recollection of Waelder's talk, provide sources for questioning orthodoxy in technique. As Waelder's idea reminds us how much more we have to learn, Wallerstein's reminds us that some of what we think we know may also be questionable. That is my main point; these are among the sources of the development of diversity in technique.

I would, however, like to stay with the support issue for a while. As a developmentalist, I find it unsurprising that some mix of support and insight would underlie structural change. The "structural changes"— the altered relations among drive, ego, and conscience—seen in the course of a child's development (where those changes are massive) undoubtedly grow out of increasing cognitive power (among other developmental changes) in settings of "supportive" relationships. That is what human psychic development is about. I recognize that such relationships must allow for autonomy as well as support, and the analytic relationship, too, does that. One need not assume a priori that change in psychoanalysis imitates developmental change, but it would be equally unwise to assume that the one does *not* give clues to the other. After all, the patient is all one person, whether growing up or lying down.

The mention of support may lead some readers to question whether what is being carried out is still "truly" analysis. It is, I firmly believe, part of what most analysts do, at least at many moments in their work. It is also built into the basic structure of the analytic arrangement through reliability, attentiveness, and a nonjudgmental stance, even though it may take a patient a long while to be able to experience support in this way. And, since we do not and cannot relentlessly interpret, often our refraining from interpretation is itself a form of support. "Support" is inescapable. In my own work I have no doubt that I am still conducting analyses when subtle or momentary, or sometimes even larger, supportive elements (again, of complex kinds) enter in. But I believe that whether this is "truly" analysis is a tired question. I have no objection to a pure definition of an ideal type—in the sense of a model—of analysis, so long as we recognize that it is not an ideal that should govern this *particular* treatment with this *particular* patient *now*. Informed flexibility in our work, and not purity of any sort, is what we need and generally have. But informed flexibility requires a full look at all of the pieces of the analytic exchange, including supportive features that may be present.

Excessive Attachments to Theories of Technique

With characteristic flair, Donald Kaplan (1990) said that the basic analytic situation is always an oedipal one since there is always a triangle in the office: the patient, the analyst, and the analyst's technique. The patient feels deprived or excluded by the analyst's loyalty and attachment to his or her theory of technique; were it not for that relationship, the patient could surely have much more of the analyst. The conditions for oedipal rivalry are built in.

The patient is right in a way. And it is not only the patient who may feel passionate about the analyst's loyalty to a theory of technique. The analyst, too, often has a countertransference to the theory of technique with which he or she operates. At worst, the analyst may cling to a particular theory of technique as though it must be the "right" way to do things, trusting that it will see the work through. Again at worst, the more problematic the treatment, the more the analyst clings to the theory of technique in this scenario, resolving doubt through belief, replacing thought with allegiance to authority. The problem is serious, particularly because the theory of technique should not be altered lightly. It has a history; it has evolved among colleagues over years; it has been tested and found useful; and alterations, no matter how rational or necessary they may seem, pose the danger that they themselves are the product of some countertransferential acting out by the analyst. The problem is not easily resolved. But the procrustean bed solution—the bed is the right size and the patient must be fitted into it—is surely not adequate. When this solution is driven by blind attachment, by submission to authority, by self-satisfied rigidity, or by any other professional or personal problem hiding as "clinical experience," loyalty to a theory of technique is countertransferential and problematic. I use the term *countertransference* here in its usual meaning(s): either as a specific reaction to the demands or difficulties with a particular patient, or as an expression of the broader character problems of a particular analyst that affect all of his or her work (A. Reich, 1951).

Addressing an aspect of this problem within the tradition of interpretation as the center of technique, Paul Meehl (1994) discusses intermittent reinforcement, a type of conditioning in which reward comes occasionally but unpredictably. Mice on this reinforcement schedule decondition very slowly: they keep pressing the bar, never knowing whether next time that food pellet will come bouncing into the cage. Meehl says: "A good Skinnerian will remind us that the interpreter of psychoanalytic material is on an intermittent reinforcement schedule and that therefore his verbal behavior and his belief system will be maintained, despite numerous extinction trials that constitute potential refuters" (p. 31). Just like mice! That is, the observed power of *some* interpretations keeps us interpreting even in the face of less than fully rewarding responses to or effects of other interpretations. I am not suggesting that interpretation should be thrown out as a technical tool. Hardly. But Meehl alerts us to one of the ways in which precious belief systems—theories of technique in this case—can be maintained no matter what. His point applies not only to interpretation but to any favorite intervention mode.

I have at times found myself torn between what I felt was needed at one point in an analysis with a particular patient, on the one hand, and my internal commands and introjects, the voices of my particular "received wisdom," on the other. Unfortunately, however, the best solution is not always on one side—either trying something new or staying with the old. There is much to be said for what has been slowly learned and tested over the years. And so, rephrasing, I have also found myself torn between what felt like my urges with regard to this or that intervention and my restraining judgment. At times I have gone one way, at times another. I have learned over the years that if I wait and listen, I learn more about what is going on with the patient. The same watchful, cautious, experimental attitude can apply to variations in technique. One learns from what one tries—errors, warts, and all. Obviously, when one works with people who have put themselves in one's care, the ground rules for and the limited nature of anything experimental must always be kept in mind. But excessive caution is a danger, too. So we come full circle, back to the danger of believing that "this is *the* way" and sticking slavishly to it.

Theories of Technique and of Mind
Our theories of mind affect what we hear in a patient's associations, altering and potentially expanding what we formulate back to the patient. The effects go beyond what we formulate, however, perhaps altering our views of how the patient should be worked with or how

the process should be conducted altogether. Thus, theories of mind affect theories of technique. Let me expand on this by drawing on an earlier discussion of this subject (Pine, 1988).[1]

While Freud placed evenly suspended attention at the core of the psychoanalytic listening process—as the way of being open to what is new, individualized, and focal in a particular patient in a given session—evenly suspended attention does not in itself guarantee such openness. It is the natural tendency of mind to make sense of things, to make order out of disorder, to seek closure. Sitting with a patient, listening to the often mystifying flow of associations, the clinician will naturally find ordering principles—red threads, meanings. Indeed, we count on this feature of mind in our clinical work. Freud's guideline of evenly suspended attention makes sense only if we recognize its counterpart in the sense-making, meaning-finding, ordering tendencies of the human mind.

Freud's idea was, of course, to allow meaning to emerge rather than be imposed by preformed notions. The clinician's mind is never blank. It is filled with personal history, his or her own analysis, the general background of what has been learned from all previous patients, prior clinical history with the present patient, and general theory. The intent of evenly suspended attention is to produce not blank minds but uncommitted and receptive ones.

Total lack of commitment is an impossibility, and the first source of the interruption of evenly suspended attention is Freud's monumental theoretical achievement itself. The creation of psychoanalytic theory, with its view of human mental functioning as organized around drives and conflict, creates basic assumptions and expectations about the potential meanings of the content of an analytic session. Thus, while we may approximate evenly suspended attention—uncommitted listening—in relation to the particular contents of a particular hour,

1. The following three paragraphs were originally published in "The Four Psychologies of Psychoanalysis," *Journal of the American Psychoanalytic Association* (1988) 36: 571–596, and are only slightly modified here.

ordinarily we have in mind a general set of theoretical constructs that dictate the *potential* meanings of what we are hearing. The array of potential meanings need not be narrow (and, indeed, even working within the classical Freudian tradition the array of possibilities feels virtually endless during the ongoing immediacy of the work), but nonetheless it is slanted in significant ways. "Uncommitted" listening occurs in the context of broader theoretical commitments regarding conceptions of personality development, personality organization, pathogenesis, and their unfolding in the treatment situation. Without such guiding concepts, we could not do the work; still, we must recognize that they create profound limitations on truly evenhanded, uncommitted listening.

Psychoanalysis has successively produced drive, ego, object relations, and self theories. These have grown from the minds of clinicians steeped in psychoanalytic work. And those diverse theories of mind have also interacted with hermeneutic, narrative, and deconstructive traditions as these have impinged on psychoanalysis. The result has been the recognition that there are many ways to tell the patient's story—in general and even in a particular session—and that the story once told does not remain fixed. The range is not unlimited; an "anything goes" formula need not be seen as the outcome. But the patient can meaningfully respond to multiple tellings of the meanings of the associations and transactions of a particular session. This is so because of the complexity of mind, because of its working through multiple functions and overdetermination, and because many features of the patient are likely to be simultaneously present in every session; such features are hierarchically organized, and different levels of the particular hierarchy then active can be meaningfully addressed.

At the same time, and in some ways contrary to the hermeneutic tradition, developmental studies have operated as a kind of basic science for psychoanalysis, simultaneously anchoring analytic concepts in real-life histories and expanding such concepts as we better understand the range of developmental happenings. Arnold Cooper (1987) puts it this way:

I would emphasize that psychoanalysis, like history but unlike fiction, does have anchoring points. History's anchoring points are the evidences that events did occur. There was a Roman Empire, it did have dates, actual persons lived and died. These "facts" place a limit on the narratives and interpretations that may seriously be entertained. Psychoanalysis is anchored in its scientific base in developmental psychology and in the biology of attachment and affects. Biology confers limits and regularities on possible histories, and our construction of the past must accord with this scientific knowledge. (pp. 83–84)

That same developmental psychology attests to the significance not only of drives and the conflicts around them but also of the emergence of the "I" and the sense of self and its frailties, the profound and endless impact of object relations and their coloring of experience, and the astonishing advances in ego development, along with the significant deformations in ego development as well. All this supports diverse views of the constituents of mind.

Work with a wider array of patients has also expanded our views of the significant features of mind. Work with the very young and the very disturbed has sometimes thrust concepts of ego, self, and object relations more forcefully into our theories. But once these aspects of mind have been recognized in this context, it is no longer possible to miss seeing them in all individuals at all levels and at all times.

These advancements at the level of theories of mind have had profound effects on theories of technique, again contributing to diversity. The effects come in at least two broad ways. First, effects are seen in how the events and ideas of a session are formulated. Formulations in terms of drives, ego, object relations, or self produce their own dynamism; they act as "suggestions," steering the subsequent content and creating a particular language of understanding within the analytic pair. They also impact the relationship in often not so subtle ways and therefore have significant effects on the development of the transference.

A second effect on technique stemming from theoretical diversity has to do with what one considers important in mental function *and how one works with it*. For example, concepts of defect and deficit as well as conflict, of object relational or ego *need* as well as drive-based *wish*, affect technique as well as formulation. And concepts regarding the centrality of object relations, while they may affect the content of interpretations first and even primarily, are also likely to affect the conception of the domain in which the significant mental content plays itself out (that is, in the "between us" in the office) as well as the conception of the relative roles of interpretation and relational features in the therapeutic impact.

Construction of the Observational Field

We have learned that the mode of observation profoundly shapes what we see in the observational field, sometimes determining even what it is that can be expressed. This awareness has fully impacted analytic thinking only in recent years. By way of introduction to related material, some years ago Theodore Lidz prefaced his book *The Person* (1968) with the observation that his intent was to help medical students overcome their narrow, mechanistic view of the person-as-organism. He explained that mechanistic view by pointing out that the medical student's first contact with a patient was through a thin slice on a microscope slide and the second contact was with a cadaver. The observational field established a certain form of connection, or nonconnection in this instance.

The issue of what one sees in a particular observational situation has also been much in the forefront for group and family therapists who make a case for the idea that those observational situations effectively emphasize certain phenomena: with families, family interactino; with groups, peer interaction and real-world adaptation. Neither set of therapists would agree that these are the *only* phenomena these situations elicit, any more than an analyst would agree that family relations and peer interactions cannot be valuably (though differently) explored through the analytic method. It may be, however, that the observational situation that favors the coming forth of certain phenomena obscures, to some degree, the coming forth of others. We analysts have favored our particular observational setup because we seek to approach the mind via intrapsychic representations and the conflicts around them. But this is just the point: the observational field affects what is observed.

The issue of the impact of the observational field arose also in psychoanalytic writings and informal discussions during the 1980s in relation to Kohut's and Kernberg's views of the place of aggression in narcissistic character. The question raised more than once was whether the more vigorous interpretation of aggression by the Kernbergian analyst tended to elicit aggression and thereby confirm the theory that it was there to begin with, and whether the more accepting and mirroring stance of the Kohutian analyst tended to attenuate or leave no room for aggression, thereby confirming its lesser salience. The truth or falsity of these speculations is not my concern here; I only make the point that recognizing the effect of the observational (and, here, the interactive) situation on the material observed is not new to us.

Probably Merton Gill more than anyone else brought these issues into the heart of psychoanalysis. It follows directly from his position that the basic trio of analytic guidelines—neutrality, abstinence, and relative anonymity—represents a particular observational stance and is in fact a *communication*, defining who the analyst is; this in turn affects the what and how of the patient's communication as well as the evolution of the transference. Gill's position was not extremist, and he makes it clear in *Psychoanalysis in Transition* (1994) that we have to work simultaneously with the views that (1) a person has an intrapsychic life that is carried along and expressed in each new situation and (2) the person is responsive to and shaped by the surrounding social characteristics.

The potential for slippery slopes or doubt and perfectionism exists on every side. If the classical analytic trio of guidelines was an attempt to rule out the analyst, thereby obscuring certain kinds of interpersonal phenomena, should the analyst be more related or self-revealing or involved? If face-to-face active interrelatedness tends to obscure certain intrapsychic phenomena, should the analyst disappear into silence? Must one always focus on the interactive and intersubjective side of clinical phenomena? On the intrapsychic side? Should we seek the Goldilocks solution—not too little, not too much, but just right? All these are hopeless attempts at solution through action. Gill's point, as I read it, is that we need to be maximally aware of the impact of our technique on the process, maximally aware of the effect of the observational conditions that we foist on the phenomena observed. The danger is in not having that awareness—no matter what the technical style, whether more removed or more related, more quiet or more active, more low-key or more forceful, more hidden or more self-revealing.

My preferred stance at this point in my work—reflecting some combination of my own analysis, what I was taught early on, what I have learned along the way, and who I am now as a person—is to have the patient use the couch if possible (as it usually is), to indicate to the patient that it is "generally best" to try to say whatever comes to mind, and to be myself as active as I judge that the situation requires or permits. I think of the couch as giving analysands the opportunity, on the one hand, to turn inward, toward their own inner life and away from me to the degree that they wish or, on the other hand, to speak to me, with me, in spite of their being on the couch. I find that they can do either if they are so impelled. I am cautiously responsive in either case, attempting to be tactful enough to be present enough (but not too much) to enable the process to get started, all the while trying to understand what the process is that is getting started. That is, I try to be aware not only of the verbally reported content but also of the tugs and avoidances, the seductions and rejections, the demands and the renunciations that the analysand lives out in relation to me. It is by no means easier to become clear about these variables early on than to be clear on issues of unconscious meaning. But I take note of what I see when I see it and am ready for the process between me and the patient or the process within the patient to take precedence at any particular time, or more so with some patients in one way or with others in other ways. I try to maintain an "equidistant" stance with regard to issues of the one-person or two-person psychology, just as I do toward the various components of the patient's intrapsychic life. None of these approaches eliminates the role of the observational situation that is my focus right now. But I try not to operate with the idea that the mode of my working is a silent constant that need not be attended to.

Analytic Change: Development and Conflict

The last of the backdrops to the current diversity in technique that I discuss here (though there are presumably others that might be added) develops from a seemingly offhand comment that I heard made by a panelist at the annual meeting of the American Psychoanalytic Association in New York several years ago. Discussions on the subject of converting psychotherapy to psychoanalysis are common; this comment, however, suggested the reverse direction. The speaker said, as an aside in the midst of some general discussion about analysis, "We all know that every psychoanalysis ends as a psychotherapy." Do we all know it? Is it true? *Every* psychoanalysis?

The statement passed by, and it was only later that I began to think about it. (Unfortunately, I do not even know the speaker's name, but my thanks to him, whoever he is.) Although I do not know what exactly the speaker had in mind, the remark has taken on a specific set of meanings for me over time. I do not feel it to hold true for every psychoanalysis in my own work, but it is true often enough to be attended to seriously. In treatment a great deal of uncovering work gets done, but nonetheless something more is often needed. Or a great deal of uncovering work gets done and the question of *change* is still very much with us and unachieved in particular areas. I am aware of the need for working through, but I am speaking of instances in which it seems that much of that has been done. Of course I am aware that there is always more that can be uncovered, and often enough that is the direction the work takes. But it also has seemed to me that this is precisely the place where countertransference to one's theory of technique may enter in, and there is the dilemma. Should one keep working as one has been working, continuing to uncover what is going on—in the belief (or faith) that that is how progress will be made? That is, do we trust the technique (whatever it may be in the particular analyst's case), to the possible detriment of the patient? Or do we shift to something else—and, if so, to what? And might that shift be beneficial or detrimental to the work? These questions admit of no simple answers, but it is perhaps an aspect of what my anonymous source had in mind with his remark that every psychoanalysis ends as a psychotherapy. Certainly that speaker and I are not alone in facing this problem, and it too must be a source of diversity in technique. It harks back to my earlier discussion of Waelder and the idea that if the analytic process always worked optimally, there would be no need for new developments in theory *or* technique.

To pursue this question of analytic change, or of a partial shift to psychotherapeutic methods of change (not in itself a clear distinction), let me draw a distinction within the multitude of insight-enhancing interpretations. The periodic complaint from a patient—"I understand it but it doesn't change"—is most frequently heard with respect to long-term phenomena: relatively fixed symptoms, long-lasting character traits, chronic affective states, and the like. The interpretations that most frequently bring about a sudden shift in the patient's state or behavior are more likely to be related to short-term phenomena: a block in the analytic process that is freed, a new symptom just emerging that disappears, a specific conflict in the patient's everyday life that is resolved, or a specific transference struggle that passes. In the sphere of long-term phenomena, interpretations may lead to the dramatic emergence of new material and even dramatic shifts in the psychological state, but usually not to dramatic (and sometimes not even to slow) change in long-lasting symptoms, character traits, or moods. This is not surprising since such long-term features are highly structuralized (however we define that). So it may be worth bearing in mind the (at times) differential effect of interpretation on short-term or process phenomena versus long-term structuralized phenomena.

This distinction returns us to Wallerstein's observations about structural change and how it comes about. But now I would like to turn the question around. Instead of the more general, unanchored question—how does structural change take place?—let us ask the more specific one—how can we bring about change in these *specific* structuralized aspects of this *particular* patient? This shift moves the question to the particular, the person-centered, the concrete. And in this domain we might well expect that different processes would be relevant, depending on the particular feature and the context (that is, the person) in which it is set. Here lies yet another seed of diversity.

An earlier discussion (Pine, 1992) sets my present discussion in a broader context.[2] In psychoanalysis, we are always dealing with at least two kinds of pathology—developmental pathology and conflict pathology (see Fonagy and Moran, 1991). Each may have somewhat different requirements for change. The two overlap and are intertwined but are conceptually distinguishable. They correspond to structure and function—that is, to the construction of the intrapsychic world (and the *developmental* failures therein) and to how that inner world then works (including a heavy dose of *conflict*). Interpretation is a relatively more effective tool in dealing with conflict pathology than with developmental pathology. While there is a lot we know and a lot we do not know about the effectiveness of interpretation with conflict pathology, we know much less about instrumentalities for bringing about change in developmental pathology. This issue is hardly new; Ferenczi's (1933), Alexander's (1956), and Balint's (1968) works were early efforts in this domain, as was Kohut's (1977) later work.

The presence of conflict is obvious. To me, the presence of defects in the development of areas of the psyche is equally obvious, given that *everything* undergoes development and can therefore develop badly or well. There is no reason to assume a priori that interpretation

2. The following four paragraphs were originally published in "From Technique to a Theory of Psychic Change," *International Journal of Psychoanalysis* (1992) 73: 251–254, and are only slightly modified here.

and insight can, in every instance, repair after the fact developmental achievements that have not come into being on their own timetable earlier on. Developmental defects are not always apparent as such because *all* aspects of a person, defects included, get caught up in conflict and have fantasies and meanings attached to them, at least secondarily. This is, in part, because everything in the person will be intrapsychically "explained" in some way—that is, will have fantasies and meanings built around it. Thus, emotional flooding was "explained" unconsciously by one patient in urinary terms, and as a sign of badness for which guilt or shame was the "appropriate" response, even though the flooding seemed to me to reflect a defect in the development of affect regulation (which itself needs to be explained). Meanings and fantasies can power behavior and thought whether or not they are the creators of those behaviors and thoughts in the first instance. Hence, clarification of such conflictual meanings will not necessarily correct the structural defects resulting from developmental failures even though such clarification is always a significant part of the work with them, potentially lessening secondary conflict and lessening interferences with compensatory functioning.

The existence of these two forms of pathology (developmental and conflictual) is inevitable and is grounded in the biology of the human being. The fact that we have a long period of development and are not capable of independent functioning at birth (in contrast to lower animals), and the fact that we are dependent in that early period on an unpredictable and often faulted human environment, guarantee that at least some aspects of every human being will not develop well. This fact *is* the fact of developmental pathology. Unreliability of object contact or object constancy, failure to tame drives or develop stable defenses, deficiencies in self-esteem, in frustration tolerance, in affect modulation, blurring of self and object boundaries—these often (though not always) reflect developmental pathology. And similarly, in terms of the biological roots of the two forms of pathology, the fact that the human brain is so complex provides the guarantee that psychic life will be filled with contradiction and cross-purposes—in short, conflict—and to this we can add the guarantees of conflict stemming from the complexities of the cultural demands on us. A familiar example of what I have in mind is Kernberg's (1975) mention of conflict involving primitive rage and primitive defenses (such as splitting): he meant the adjective *primitive* to say that the parties to the *conflict* pathology are themselves reflective of pathological *developmental* failures.

While we have all had experiences with both the effectiveness and the failings of interpretation of conflict, we are less experienced with approaches to the developmental pathologies, or even to their conceptualization. Problems such as these underlie the growth of diversity in technique in efforts to grapple with the problem. Technical concepts such as empathy, the holding environment, containment, and corrective emotional experience (or corrective object relationship) are relevant here. However, there is so much ideologically driven dispute with regard to such concepts in the literature that we have not yet had a chance to see that they, too, are unlikely to have any one-to-one relation to psychic change. I suspect that they would have to be specified much more precisely. For example, while I find it reasonable to expect that empathic understanding will be valuable to a person who grew up not heard, or not mattering, or used by another for the other's purposes, it is not at all clear that empathic understanding (beyond its place as ordinary human decency) is specifically change-relevant for developmental failures—say, in the effectiveness of defense, or affect flooding, or lacunae in conscience. It seems to me likely that quite varied approaches to quite varied developmental pathologies will have some place. I have described some specifics of such work earlier (Pine, 1985, 1990). In my experience in working with patients with aberrant development of self-other differentiation, much valuable work seemed to be accomplished via interpretation, probably because here interpretation in the transference is indissolubly linked to experiencing in the patient-analyst relationship and, I believe, because interpretation wakes the patient up to the experience of the maintenance of boundaries even in the setting of profound intimacy.

Concluding Remarks

In this chapter, I have roved widely to give the reader a sense of some of the many considerations that form the clinical and intellectual back-drop to diversity in technique. I have used six different ideas as my starting points: Waelder's comment that insufficiencies in the effectiveness of our clinical methods propel new formulations in theory—and, I added, in technique; Wallerstein's finding that all insight treatment includes significant supportive features and that both these features and the work of insight are related to "structural change," a finding that challenges some of our conventional wisdom; the analyst's countertransference to a theory of technique and the dangers and limitations therein, though counterbalanced by the rational bases for caution about change in technique; the proliferation of models of mind with their implications for technique and for how, more broadly, the person, the illness, and the psychoanalytic process are understood; the effect on the data of psychoanalysis of the observational position and the slippery slopes and self-doubts that can impose themselves on the analyst's task as a result of understanding this effect; and the implications for technique of the partial contrast between the developmental and the conflict pathologies, each with its own clinical demands and uncertainties.

These considerations both underlie the evolution of diversity in technique and undercut any reach for orthodoxy, whatever the particular orthodoxy may be. Much about the uncertainties of the psychoanalytic clinician's work makes an orthodoxy—a source of certainty—appealing, but there is much in at least some of our patients that would catch us up short if we found ourselves listening more to our rules than to their voices.

Psychoanalysis is a highly individual activity, shaped by the personal history, character, and professional training of each practitioner and generally modified over time by clinical experience. Out of this mix, each analyst develops an individual way of working, which is of course necessary if chaos is not to reign. Nonetheless, the offerings on the table of psychoanalytic theory and technique give us a rich array to work with. I see it as advantageous for each practitioner to use the full array to the degree possible as circumstances require. My impression is that different issues come to the fore with different patients— not only in terms of meanings and content but in the domain in which the work happens, be this past, outside present, transference, or here-and-now. And this is a *patient* variable as well as, potentially, an *analyst* variable. Some patients seem to locate the work primarily intrapsychically, while others seem to pull for interrelatedness or for getting inside the analyst's subjectivity. These are real differences among analysands, not simply "resistances" to working in some other way, although they may be that, too. Just as the phenomena of drive, ego function, object relations, and self exist in everyone and are hierarchically arranged in endlessly varied and individualized ways (Pine, 1990), so too are the patient's responsiveness to or pulls toward one or another kind of intervention. The choice is wide ranging but probably hierarchically organized so that this or that approach is the most effective one with this patient at this time—changing with different patients and probably also changing at different times with each one.

Diversity can be seen as breeding confusion or bringing riches; I lean toward the latter position. In Part II, I discuss a variety of more specific issues within the widely diversified domain of psychoanalytic technique. Each issue is focused and concrete. The issues do not add up to a general theory of technique. The work is in the details, and the details keep shifting as the clinical moment changes. But before I turn to that discussion, I want to expand on the development of diversity in psychoanalytic theories of mind and then return to their implications for technique.

2 Diversity in Theory: One Psychoanalysis Composed of Many

Although Hartmann (1964) proposed that psychoanalysis be seen as a general psychology, that reach is perhaps too great. There are too many issues in the domains of perception, learning, development, and group process, for example, that are well beyond the attention and grasp of psychoanalysis—though psychoanalysis may contribute something to their understanding. But psychoanalysis must aspire to be a general psychology of the phenomena of the psychoanalytic situation, of the human mind as it is seen through the lens of the psychoanalytic process.

That lens is subject to the coloration brought to it by the mind of the observer. It is inevitable that reports in the literature will be some mix of the data of the observed and self-observing analysand and the

I want to thank Dr. Robert Wallerstein for allowing me to use this paraphrase of his title, "One Psychoanalysis or Many" (Wallerstein, 1988).

observing, responsive, and self-expressing analyst. Those, we now recognize, *are* the data of psychoanalysis. Given that interactive and interpretive aspect of the data, the psychoanalytic situation (patient on couch, frequent sessions, free association) provides a magnificent observational opportunity, and analysts, by and large, have learned to be careful observers.

Analysts' observations have been variously described in terms of (1) relations among sexual and aggressive urges, defenses against them, and the demands of conscience—relations characterized by conflict and attempts at its resolution through compromise; (2) a mind populated by incorporated object images shaped by wish, affect, and fantasy and characterized by repetition and externalization of the relations with early objects; and (3) painful subjective states of self-experience characterized by issues around personal boundaries and esteem, narcissistic pain, and efforts at both compensation for and endless continuance of the painful state. These diverse views are bound together as "psychoanalytic" by their grounding in early bodily and object relational experiences, the role of unconscious mental functioning, which follows different rules from directed rational thought, and the centrality of painful affect and attempts to cope with it (Jacobson, 1994). A general psychology of the psychoanalytic situation must find a significant place for each of these observations and formulations.

Diversity is a fact of contemporary psychoanalytic theory. Killingmo (1985a) writes: "In clinical practice concepts from the different frames of reference [of drive, ego, object relations, and self] are used interchangeably without causing too much controversy. However, this smooth functioning on the clinical level seems to be possible only because the inherent theoretical conflicts between the different positions are not made explicit" (p. 54). He goes on to make these theoretical conflicts explicit and later (1985b) attempts a reconciliation through ideas regarding organizing functions of the ego.

A way both to respect and to accommodate the diversity is required. My approach (Pine, 1985, 1988, 1990) has been to emphasize integration, not at the level of general theory but at the level of clinical theory, "experience-near" with respect to phenomena of individual lives, and to recognize that all the phenomena (of drive, ego function, object relations, and self-experience) are formative developmentally and active clinically at different moments. I have attempted to show that the development of an array of motivations and the organization of the many phenomena in "personal hierarchies" differ in each individual. The spirit is that of Rangell's (1983) call for a cumulative "total psychoanalytic theory" (p. 861).

In the subsequent sections of this chapter, I first review the development of a broadened psychoanalytic theory in ways that highlight its organic growth. To establish the place of the full theoretical array as a usable context for ongoing clinical work, I also outline several routes to integration within the broadened theory. Second, I discuss and respond to three critiques that can be leveled against the approach: the danger of internally contradictory eclecticism, the questionable extricability of psychoanalytic formulations from the theories of which they are a part, and—specifically tied to the aims of this book—the issue of clinical confusion, or how one decides which view of the mind one "should" be working with clinically at any specific point. (This last point is extensively illustrated in Chapter 7.) And third, I apply the model to a selection of current issues in psychoanalysis, attempting to show its value for clinical work and for the clinical and developmental theories that provide its foundations. Overall, my aim is to expand the discussion of diversity in theory as it underlies the development of diversity in technique.

An Expanded and Integrated Psychoanalysis
It is easy to look at the expansion of psychoanalytic theories (from their birth in a radical new drive theory to their proliferation in psychologies of ego, object relations, and self) in terms of strong charismatic leaders, on the one hand, and group loyalties and intergroup rivalries, on the other. While it would be enlightening to do so, to consider this the full story would be clearly a mistake. It would be divisive, by ignoring the fact that all these views are already represented

in Freud's own writings, for the most part explicitly. Furthermore, it would be tendentious, by ignoring the fact that each of the intellectual leaders and the groups around them worked with ideas based on observations and formulations emanating from their psychoanalytic work.

Culture- or personality-driven changes are better viewed in terms of a rational organic growth of psychoanalytic theory—rational in that it reflects achieved understandings of psychoanalytic data, organic in that it can be seen (from the perspective of time) to reflect a logical, inevitable expansion in necessary directions. And though the seeds can be found in Freud's writings, these other views reflect major expansions of theory, just as Freud himself radically altered and expanded his views over time.

In pursuing this approach to the evolution of psychoanalytic theory, recognition will be given to conceptual requirements of the theory itself, new ways of understanding clinical data (and at times, new data), additional methods of observing relevant data (child analysis, infant and child observations), and a broad perspective from an elementary evolutionary biology. I use the idea presented elsewhere (Pine, 1990) of four psychologies of psychoanalysis (drive, ego, object, self)—a "psychology" being a view of the way mental life is motivated and organized—but here I emphasize integration—the development of one overall psychoanalytic psychology of mind.

Under the influence of the discoveries of his self-analysis combined with observations of his patients, Freud (1905) fairly rapidly developed a view of the mind centered around sexual (and, later, aggressive) drives. There was, of course, much more to his theories, but this was a central, a controversial, and indeed a grand conception. In the background, and no doubt influencing Freud's move in this direction, was the sexually repressive culture of his middle-class Vienna, which underlay the pathological instances he encountered. Also, in science, a Newtonian worldview prevailed, a world of force and counterforce, of predictable energy transformations, into which a theory of instinctual drive versus defenses, of cathexis and countercathexis, of libidinal energies, readily fit. In perspective, however, the ultimate justification for a drive psychology is our position in evolution: we are *all animals*, and we share with other animals the thrust for sexual activity, which guarantees reproduction and survival of the species and which we know interplays with pleasure and power in ways that evolution built in to insure sexual performance. We also share aggression in the service of territoriality (which among humans includes psychic as well as bodily space) and in the service of food-getting (seen in the infant's vigorous cry when unsatisfied or the potential for rage at all ages with acutely experienced nonsatisfaction). These impulses are represented psychically and in an infinite number of transformed guises.

A drive psychology goes a long way toward clarifying human motivation and human relationships. In the inevitable clash of psychological urges with the requirements of communal living (Freud, 1930) and the inevitable internal clash between opposing impulses toward the same object, we find the basis for understanding a great deal about the centrality of conflict and the evolution of intrapsychic defense. The psychic representation of biological drives enriches the mind and underlies our view of the complexity of psychic life, as the concept of sublimation expands our view of motivation. From early on, the libidinal drives were used to explain characterology (Abraham, 1921, 1924; Freud, 1908) and anxiety (Freud, 1916–17), then seen as a transformation of libidinal energy. The view has substantial explanatory power.

But a psychology of ego function—of defense, adaptation, and reality testing—was indispensable and existed from the beginning in Freud's (1894) concepts of defense and repression, without which he could not explain his clinical observations. Ultimately the internal requirements of Freud's theory led to an ego psychology. Since the system Unconscious and, later, the id are timeless and do not learn, some apparatus was needed to explain learning and change, in life as well as in the psychoanalytic process itself. Within the theory, the ego did this job. It was no accident that an early extensive view of ego function was produced by a child analyst, Anna Freud (1936), since observation of children so powerfully reveals the profound expansions of the domain of the ego. But, again, the final justification for a psychology of ego function is our position in evolution: we are *partially preadapted*. Our adaptation to the environment is not complete at birth; behavior is not fully governed by instinctual automatisms; we are dependent on caretakers to negotiate survival. We are not outside of evolution, however, and evolution would not have produced a creature with no adaptive capacities; that would not serve survival of the species. This idea informs Hartmann's (1939) concept of ego apparatuses, the biologically built-in tools for adaptation through ego function: perception, memory, affect, motility, and thought.

A psychology of the ego enriches understanding of the other (non-drive) side of conflict and underlies the positive view of "resistance"; that is, the mind of the patient is not simply resisting something else, which is the "important" something, but is revealing itself, revealing the patient's mode of functioning intrapsychically. Starting with Reich (1949), the understanding of characterology expanded to include ego mechanisms, characteristic defensive styles. Freud (1926) reconceptualized anxiety, in particular the anxiety signal that triggers automatic defenses, as a developed tool of ego function. And, since the tools of ego function develop over time and can develop poorly or well, we have the conceptual basis for phenomena of ego defect (Pine, 1990): failures in, say, the anxiety signal (such that overwhelming anxiety arises rapidly), or in impulse control, or object constancy, or the development of reliable defenses, or affect modulation—any of which can vastly heighten the difficulty of moving forward in a particular patient's psychoanalysis.

The foundations of both the drives and the ego apparatuses are built in biologically. The turn to the study of object relations can now be seen as inevitable. It is the other half of the complemental series— the sources of development and psychopathology not only in the intrinsic unfolding of the biologically built-in programs but also in unique and adventitious experiences with caretakers. It is the other side of the nature-nurture controversy. Clinical work, which centers so much on the patient's relations to his or her significant (internal and external) objects, naturally produced attempts at systematic (not just uniquely experiential) understandings of object relations; this systematizing attempt *is* object relations theory. In addition, child and especially infant observation, where access to fantasies is not possible but observation of actual relations is compelling, also produced movement toward the inclusion of object relations theories in the psychoanalytic lexicon. But once again, the ultimate justification for an object relations theory is our position in evolution: we are partially preadapted, but only partially. Therefore, we are dependent on objects—our primary caretakers—for long years in order to insure survival. This fact guarantees the impact of those caretakers on the psychic life of the individual. Object relations theory is the attempt to view that impact systematically and psychoanalytically.[1]

Object relations concepts underlie Freud's views of transference, identification, superego formation, and the Oedipus complex; they are inescapable and have been part of psychoanalysis from the start, although, like the ego, received full systematic recognition only later on. Through our study of identification, they help us understand character, defensive style, and the choice of sublimations. They have also given us a view of the "representational world" (Sandler and Rosenblatt, 1962), the internal map that develops progressively and governs our expectancies with regard to human relationships, and to which we assimilate ongoing relationships (Piaget, 1952)—that is, reading them in terms of the schema of expectancies based on past experience. This assimilation of new experience into the internal map of expectancies underlies the repetitiveness of object relations.

Just as the study of drives inevitably produced a focus on the defenses of the ego, the study of object relations did the same for

---

1. Object relations theory as I understand it is a view of the mind's workings and of how the mind is constituted. In the United States, however, it is often described critically as a view of how change takes place (the holding environment, the new object relationship). Whatever my thoughts on the latter, it is the former position I am discussing here.

the self. It is no accident that, historically, the three most prominent psychoanalytic infant observers, each of whom examined early mother-infant relations, also found it necessary to write in terms of the development of "self" (for example, Spitz, 1957; Winnicott, 1960; Mahler, 1972). Clinical observations, especially of certain kinds of patients (Kohut, 1971, 1977), have also pushed in that direction. But, once again, the justification for a psychology of self is our position in evolution: we are not only animals but *self-conscious* animals. That is, our developed brain and consciousness are such that we carry experience, reflect on it, and endow it with meaning; we are aware of subjective states, and, when they are not working well, we suffer them. Such ideas as these underlie psychologies of self.

This raises the question of where we might see primary "self" phenomena, phenomena beyond those tied to the more clear-cut, distinct ones of drive, ego, and object relations. "Primary" here may refer to early phenomena but more important (to justify the inclusion of a fourth perspective) it should mean "not secondary"—that is, not derived from something else. Thus, it is not merely a conception of self that is, for example, a compromise formation reflecting drive and defense. Subjective states of continuity, esteem, agency, and boundaries—and the emergence of "I" and self-awareness itself—are among those that writers in this area have pointed to.

It also may be useful to think in terms of ways of feeling that are built in so early that words do not express them and that are then taken for granted as what life simply is (that is, subjective states of self) (see Bollas, 1987; Bach, 1994). Like the unconscious fantasy (Arlow, 1969a, 1969b) in its ubiquity, but quite different from it in terms of its source and degree of articulation, an ongoing inner subjective state in each of us serves as a filter through which we experience the world—our personal tinted glasses, as it were. Typically these subjective states are organized around worth, continuity, wholeness, and well-being, on one side; around boundaries, realness, agency, and individuality, on another; and around comfort or basic anxiety and dis-ease, on yet another. So the tinted glasses through which each of us sees the world may be cheerily golden, denyingly rose-colored, or depressively blue or black; they may be self-definingly clear or regressively vague and undifferentiated; or, again, invitingly wide-angled or warily focused. While there may be later routes to such states as well, through conflict and compromise formation, early templates of experience lay down such states uniquely in each of us, so early and so subtly that they are ordinarily never named or identified. Yet they are likely to affect profoundly both the inner world that is constructed over time and every aspect of the way ongoing life is experienced. Earlier (Pine, 1982) I discussed this view with the proposal that, when the "I," the sense of a self, emerges early on, it does not emerge unencumbered; it is a not a blank-slate self. Rather, that "I" is immediately experienced in terms of the collection of inner affective states that have been the characteristic ones for that child; now, for good or ill, they are owned as part of that "I."

These may be among the primary "self" phenomena of human mental function. In Chapter 6, in a discussion of certain failures of the environmental provision that leave a direct, immediate, and lasting sense of a "raw wound," a wound that is forever subject to pain when re-irritated, I discuss yet another possible primary self phenomenon.

The term *self* eludes precise definition, and the phenomena to which it refers require some nailing down. But we do not seem to be able to do without the term.

Routes to Integration

How are we to integrate the diversity in current psychoanalytic theories? Three routes are available.

The Developmental Route

Kernberg (1976) has proposed that the development of mental life involves the laying down in memory of "units of experience," these experiences involving self and other around some affect (for example, the infant crying in hunger and the mother feeding). I propose adding that the other can be varyingly present (though probably never fully absent psychically), as when the infant is alone with its bodily sensations or making things happen in the world (such as squeezing a soft toy and creating a sound). Thus there are units of experience composed primarily of self and affect as well as self-other-affect. I further propose that these "units" are organized around phenomena that might be termed, at varying times, "drive," "ego," "object relations," or "self experience." The building blocks of psychic life exist in the same array of areas that psychoanalytic clinicians and theorists have been addressing.

Nothing is static in mental life, however, and all these "units of experience" (and the associated memories, expectations, wishes, fears) become interconnected. They are active, affective mini-organizations, and as such they are assimilated to other such organizations (memories) in the very act of being recorded; they color subsequent experiences as *they* are being recorded. Integration of what we, conceptually and from the outside, refer to as phenomena of drive, ego, object relations, and self is, experientially and from the inside, simply a fact of development. All forming and existing in one person, the phenomena of our several psychologies become interconnected under the sway of whichever motives and meaning systems come to exert greater or lesser dominance in that psychic life. Integration, here, is not a meta-theoretical attempt to coordinate concepts advanced by diverse theorists. It is, rather, a developmental event in which diverse phenomena of at least the several sorts I have been addressing become interconnected in each person in unique ways. It does produce a *task* for theorists, however, and that is to find ways of representing the diversity of formative events conceptually. This leads to a second approach to integration.

The Characterological Route

As an approach to integration, characterology involves clinical and structural concepts that explain how diverse aspects of a person are organized in his or her particular mental life. Psychoanalysis has various characterologies, and I do not mean to replace them. But the presence of diverse phenomena in mental life invites some attempt to produce a characterology that addresses their organization within each individual.

Elsewhere (Pine, 1990) I have put forth and illustrated a concept of personal hierarchies. It is modeled after Freud's (1905) hierarchical conception of the relations between pregenital and genital sexuality. That is, pregenital sexual wishes (oral, anal, voyeuristic, exhibitionistic, sadistic, masochistic) find their place in foreplay, hierarchically subordinated to the final aim of heterosexual genital intercourse. In this view perversions—the dominance of one or another pregenital aim, or shifts of the primary object—reflect alternative hierarchical arrangements, seen as pathological.

The phenomena of drive, ego function, object relations, and self experience are also arranged in a different hierarchy in every individual; however, there is no single "healthy" or developmentally advanced hierarchical arrangement. Pathology or adequate function can be seen in a variety of arrangements. To illustrate this simply (with regard to pathology) in terms of our familiar diagnostic schema, we could say that narcissistic disorder reflects the centrality of self issues in the hierarchy, obsessive-compulsive disorder the centrality of drive-defense issues, and "fate neurosis" (Deutsch, 1930) the centrality of repetitive object relational issues. I have given fuller clinical examples elsewhere (Pine, 1990).

A corollary of the hierarchy conception is that all these phenomena exist in every individual, but some of them at "lower" (less central) positions in the personal hierarchy. They become organized in the familiar ways we think of as overdetermination and multiple function (Waelder, 1936), each finding its way into all significant aspects of a person's functioning. Thus the child's relation to its mother comes to be shaped by wishes, defenses, and repetitive object and self experiences, and serves functions with respect to each of them. Similarly, any major pursuit—such as writing psychoanalytic papers or working as a clinical psychoanalyst—comes to serve functions with respect to drives, ego, object relations, and sense of self. Development is the process of the formation of tightly linked, hierarchically arranged organizations of phenomena of these several sorts.

The presence of these phenomena in the life history and current organization of every individual leads to a third approach to integration.

The Technical Route

Rangell's view of a cumulative "total psychoanalytic theory," in which he rejects a "cafeteria of paradigms" and "perhaps even a different theory for each patient" (1983, p. 862), would seem also to reject a different technique for each patient had he chosen to extend his statement in that direction.

Another approach is possible: not a different theory or technique for each patient, but recognition that all the phenomena spanning drive, ego, object relations, self are active components of psychic life as seen from the analytic couch and that, therefore, varieties of "content" (motives, "units of experience," "mechanisms") have to be addressed. I do not believe that different "contents" of the mind require the use of different techniques—for example, interpretation for drive-defense conflict, empathic listening for "self" issues, interactive or supportive approaches (or a focus on projective identification) for object relational phenomena. This is caricature. In any event, the "contents" do not come in unitary packages; as already noted, all are intermixed in the adult analysand, and at any one point we may not be sure what we are dealing with or what it will evolve into. Nevertheless, not only interpretation but quiet listening, redescription of what the patient has said, reconstruction, interpretation "upward," self-disclosure within the process, and other interventions may each have their place at moments, governed by what we loosely call timing and tact, and representing our best judgment at the time regarding the total clinical situation. This approach does not follow the lines of drive-ego-object-self but rather of the overall, as well as the momentary, organization of the analysand's functioning.

It will not do to define psychoanalysis as the approach to intrapsychic drive-defense conflict by means of interpretation because that does not sufficiently encompass the problematic phenomena of psychic life as heard from the couch or the broad array of technical interventions analysts regularly draw on. It will not do either to argue that psychoanalysis is best reserved for those patients who bring us only certain kinds of psychodynamic issues; *all* patients may well bring *all* the issues, even if some are less central in their particular personal hierarchy. In any event, we cannot tell in advance which issues will surface and achieve centrality during a particular analysis once begun. From this standpoint, "integration" (here, a broad range of clinical thinking, casting a wide net) is a necessity for listening and technique in the psychoanalytic situation if we are to do justice to the phenomenological range.

Critique and Response

Various critiques might be directed at the ideas thus far presented; I address three of them.

Eclecticism

While an eclectic approach at its best can involve the thoughtful integration of diverse ideas from various sources, when the term is used critically, it usually implies a random or inconsistent or internally contradictory collection of ideas. This latter approach would not be a gain, nor is it my aim.

Observations and concepts can be drawn from different psychoanalytic models as long as one takes care not to follow those models into systematic or exclusionary modes. The systematic mode says, "this is the way everything fits together." The exclusionary mode adds, "this way and no other way." It is not necessary to follow either of these modes, nor is psychoanalytic theory at a point where such could be justified. Most clinicians attempting to cope with the exigencies of everyday practice readily use an idea from here and an idea from there as needed to foster the progress of their work, without concern (or even awareness) that they are shifting between models. Some theorists have found new ways to view the phenomena of the psychoanalytic situation (for example, in terms of object relations or self issues)—just as Freud did at the outset with regard to primary sexual motives and defenses against them—and then have built complex superstructures of ideas on top of these observations. One can join any particular observer-theorist in terms of the primary observations (themselves inevitably colored by theory, of course) without following the theorist wherever he or she chooses to take the observations. Thus one can respect "self" as a useful concept, and empathy and narcissistic woundedness as apt descriptions of aspects of the clinical process, without following Kohut (1977) into his ideas regarding the "bipolar" or "superordinate" self. The same is true for other theorists, including Freud.

From another standpoint, I am proposing at least the beginnings of an integrated theory. It looks eclectic only when one starts from the point of view of already developed systematic theories. Killingmo (1985a) argues that a blending of these theories is not possible. But I have suggested that these many things *are* the phenomena of the psychoanalytic situation and turn out to be the phenomena of the developmental process as well (Pine, 1990). The questions, then, necessarily arise as to what theory might be formed around them and how might the diverse phenomena fit together and be organized. I have suggested that they come together developmentally as different experiences are reencountered by the child in new contexts and are endowed with new meanings, such that overdetermination and multiple function come to characterize all mental events—all the "units of experience" of whatever sort. They are then seen in a unique personal integration in every individual, where the phenomena of drive, ego, object relations, and self experience are organized hierarchically, one or another being more central at different moments, or at different phases of the analysis, or in different persons.

Extricability

Are psychoanalytic propositions extricable from the larger theories of which they are a part, or are they inevitably bound to those theories? Can we pick and choose an idea here, an idea there, or does that do violence to the idea?

In a discussion of my book *Drive, Ego, Object, and Self,* Berman

(1991) stated his regret (humorously) that I stopped with only four theories. He suggested that psychoanalysis has multitudes of "mini-theories" but that we do not know how to put them all together; trying to put them together is where we go wrong. Thus (in my words now) we know something about identification with lost objects, about sublimation of sexual wishes, about the sense of narcissistic injury, about reaction formations against taboo impulses, about the omnipresence of guilt, about inducing moods in the analyst in the transference-countertransference exchange, about "as-if" functioning (Deutsch, 1942) and other kinds of "false self" (Winnicott, 1960) presentations, and so on. We just do not have a theory that adequately ties them all together. From this viewpoint, extracting observations and concepts from larger theoretical contexts may not be the principal problem; rather, it is the attempt to create that larger theoretical context that is the problem. We can, and many of us do, routinely draw on clinical concepts with varying intellectual ancestry.

The following exchange between Modell (1994) and myself (Pine, 1994b) bears on both the eclecticism and the extricability issues. Modell asked how one can reconcile Kohut's (1977) and Winnicott's (1960) and Hartmann's (1950) ideas regarding a "self"; does one not run into contradiction? My response was that they each address different phenomena but use the same or related words (self, true and false self, self-representation) and lodge them in more encompassing theories. We can choose to highlight the phenomena they attempt to describe, find each of them in accord with our clinical experience (or not), use each of them in our work (or not), and adopt the larger theoretical contexts (or not). I said, still in response to Modell, that the subjective experience we call "self" can have different fault lines—those, for example, referred to by Winnicott as formed false selves and a loss of genuineness, and those referred to by Kohut as feelings of emptiness, discontinuity, or lack of cohesion—and perhaps more (such as a blurring of boundaries, an elevation of grandiosity, the absence of a sense of agency). These are additive, not contradictory concepts. In addition, each person has an *idea* of "self" (a representation within the ego), an idea that is ordinarily a compromise formation compounded of wish, defense, and ideal. Everything in human experience—bodily states, subjective mental states, stimulus inputs—receives cognitive representation. That is simply in the nature of the human mind. The presence of self-representations does not cancel the subjective experiences just listed. We can also speak of the pathology of representations. They may, for example, be unrealistic, so idealized or debased as to guarantee experience of failure or pain; they may be constructed by excluding, for example, sexuality, aggression, neediness, or autonomy, such that a continuing struggle to exclude them will always be present.

These ideas are all extricable from the theories of the person who first formulated them, and they are additive. There is nothing contradictory here, or even inconsistent. Taken together they enrich our clinical understanding of the pathology of the "self," in fact helping us to define what we mean by "self" in particular instances.

Clinical Confusion

How does one choose which "model" (drive, ego, object, self) one works with at any particular time with any particular patient? Gedo (1994) raises this question about my prior writings, suggesting (as though it were a fault) that only clinical intuition permits one to find one's way. But this comment is disingenuous: in our work we always face choices about how to respond, or whether to respond at all. The problem does not go away when one is working within a single model.

Let us imagine that one works within the so-called classical American ego psychological-structural point of view. How does one choose whether to interpret in the transference, the current life, or the reconstructed past? How does one decide whether to focus on the preoedipal or oedipal aspects of the material? The negative or positive oedipal? The defense or what seems to be defended against? Whether to be silent and not respond? It is not as though, working within a single theoretical frame, be it ego psychology, Kleinian or Kohutian theory, or any other method, the analyst's response is ever self-evident in an analysis. In contrast, we have all read or heard case presentations that seemed mechanistic because a particular analyst did "know"—from a theory—how to respond. That is not the approach to take.

The response to Gedo's question about how we choose to respond (and the response is the same for a broad-ranging multimodel theoretical view as for a more focal single view) is simply: "It all depends." It depends on the patient's tone, affect, and associations, and the prior history of the analysis up to that point. We have some guiding "rules" of technique (surface before depth, resistance before the resisted), but these are at best general guidelines, and the question of what is "surface" or "resistance" is itself rarely self-evident and changes from moment to moment. As Isakower (1965) used to say, "If you have too many rules of thumb, you will be all thumbs." There is no way for the psychoanalyst to escape responsibility for using his or her best judgment regarding response. One is best prepared for this by being maximally aware of what other analysts have discovered about the multiple, unending variants of mind.

Applications

The Clinical Application

A broadened theoretical perspective provides the conceptual basis for a more balanced technique, shaped to the individual patient and the particular clinical moment. This flexibility includes variations in the contents focused on, the locus of the work (in the patient's mind, in the past, in the transference, in the interaction), and the mode of intervention. A unifying perspective may be useful at some points, and a diverse range of possibilities at others. Though each analyst may have an intellectually or characterologically based preference for unification or diversity, patient differences and aspects of mind in general require a flexible theory. An example from my clinical work illustrates this point.

Early on in my psychoanalytic work I made a personal discovery. With a number of patients I had done a good deal of interpretive work on drive-defense constellations, and the patients seemed to understand well how their minds worked around these. But little changed (in the instances I am addressing) until I focused on the idea that the whole drive-defense arrangement was also a form of connection to the parents-of-childhood, to (however faulted) the only parents the patient ever had, to parents that he or she was reluctant to let go of. The focus on the drive-defense constellations *and* on the object relational functions (though not necessarily in that order) seemed to provide a fuller and more freeing analysis. This discovery actually drew from a theoretical tradition different from the structural theory, though I did not know that at the time.

Recently, in supervisions of students, I have had the reverse experience. The supervisees show me (in their process notes) how, again and again, they show the patient that he or she is repeating some actual, distorted, or wished-for relationship with the parent, in passive or active-reversing form. Patients are very receptive to such interpretations; they provide a sense of "fit" and, by seeming to show that a relational pattern emanated from the outside, relieve a degree of guilt. Such interventions can be enlightening and necessary. But I have found it extremely helpful to show the supervisees how they were missing (or colluding with the patient in avoiding) unconscious sexual or aggressive wishes in the patient that underlay the repetitive object relations. Here, then, was the other side of the coin. An undue emphasis on either the drive or the repetitive object relational components of psychic life, to the exclusion of the other, gives an incomplete analysis.

Another instance stems from an examination of the work of Paul Gray (1994). His central point is that one can stay close to the analytic surface and thus work with material of which the patient can readily become aware if one listens for the drive derivatives in the patient's associations and then takes note (to oneself and to the patient) of the patient's flight from, undoing of, reaction against, or other resistance to that content. This is a strong, clear, consistent view. But it assumes that the relations between drive derivatives and defenses are the principal contents of an analysis. I believe they are central, but the repetitive object relations experiences growing out of strain trauma from the childhood era, or painful subjective states of self organized around deficits in parental care, or feelings of humiliation or helplessness in relation to defects in ego function, and the interconnections of all these also need to be heard. Gray deals with this by saying that "widened scope patients" may need some approach different from what he is suggesting. But *that* approach creates a different technique for different types of patients. I believe that patients in the neurotic range and patients in the widened scope (Stone, 1954) require a wide range of interventions, because they have contended intrapsychically (sometimes unsuccessfully) with issues around drive, ego function, object relations, and self during the course of their development. Both "widened scope" patients and "Kohutian" patients—granted that these are caricatures—need interpretive work around drives and defenses (in addition to whatever else they may need), and neurotic patients at times need an empathic focus on trauma, psychic pain, or deficit. And all will inevitably bring their history of, and actions in relation to, significant objects into the transference. Patients do not come in neat categories. All minds bring all issues, to varying degrees and with differing hierarchical centrality. We cannot know fully in advance what the requirements of a particular analysis will be, but a broad approach provides the greatest possibility of hearing the patient in his or her individuality.

I recall two other instances regarding the occasional opposition between focus and balance. In recent years I have read and heard many clinical presentations by members of the British Kleinian group and have been struck by what seemed at times to be an excessive, repetitive, and sometimes presumptive (rather than evidential) use of the concept "projective identification." The concept is a powerful one, intersecting with what I understand to be the centrality of boundary issues in the course of development—one underpinning for thinking about a defense that unconsciously "exchanges" content back and forth between persons. In addition, projective identification is consistent with the current movement toward seeing the analytic situation in terms of a two-person psychology (Gill, 1994). Nonetheless, the concept can be used excessively, with the danger that it becomes an assumption rather than a discovery in clinical work and that it blocks out other understandings of defense in the clinical material. Substantially parallel comments can be made regarding Kohut's (1971, 1977, 1984) contributions. Several years ago I lost two analytic patients abruptly and came to feel that I understood what went wrong only years later, when I was able to appreciate Kohut's writings. I find that an alertness to narcissistic "raw wounds" and a less interpretive, more descriptive-empathic approach have their place centrally with some patients and to a degree with all patients. But, in my clinical judgment, I have not come across a patient to whom the full panoply of psychic mechanisms and technical approaches was not relevant. There is no patient who needs, for example, a unitary "self-psychological" approach, or a unitary any other approach, for that matter.

Different theories of mind make us receptive to, or even press us toward, particular technical approaches and a focus on particular contents and mechanisms. A broader view of mind can provide the conceptual foundations for a greater balance and breadth in technique—potentially for *every* patient, not just this for this one and that for that one. Our work and our patients gain from this approach.

The Theoretical Application

A broad theoretical reach encourages an expansion of core concepts throughout psychoanalytic theory. In 1981 Sandler, establishing a place for a wide range of personal wishes (including safety and varied wished-for role relationships), attempted to put excessive reliance on sexual and aggressive motives into perspective: "Because psychoanalytic theory and practice have placed so much emphasis on sexual and aggressive wishes, and because psychoanalysis has had to defend its findings in regard to the prevalence of such wishes, there has been a tendency to see all wishes as instinctual. With developments in ego psychology . . . psychoanalytic theoreticians have gone through the most tremendous intellectual contortions to try to derive *all* wishes from sexual and aggressive impulses" (p. 187).

A theory that fits the data gathered in the psychoanalytic situation to date has to recognize a broad array of central motives, and an expanded theoretical view points to at least some of them. Thus, with respect to sexual and aggressive impulses, broadly defined, there come to be a range of psychically represented wishes, taking direct, sublimated, displaced, aim-inhibited, or otherwise altered forms, their specific form and content shaped by personal history. This is a "proactive" motivation; it tends (through the motivating force of wishes) to "drive" behavior in particular directions. With respect to object relations, the individual tends to repeat old, now internalized, object relationships, in active or passive variants (doing or being done to, acting or eliciting). These repetitions derive their force from the pleasure associated with those early relationships (actual, imagined, or wished-for), from the strain trauma (Kris, 1956) associated with them (and therefore everlasting attempts at mastery through repetition, attempts that have gone awry and gotten stuck), and most frequently *both* the pleasure and the trauma. Both act as motives; this, too, is a proactive motive. In the sphere of defensive-adaptive (ego) function, the person clings to old solutions to internal conflict, solutions that have been achieved as ways of warding off negative affect of one sort or another and are therefore not given up easily; this is a homeostatic motive, seen in the rigidities of character style and the implacability of resistances. In the sphere of subjective states of the self, the person tends both to flee from and to cling to painful subjective states, the clinging because they are self-defining and continue relationships from the past, however unsatisfying, now experienced as internal subjective states; in the clinging aspect, this, too, is a homeostatic motivation.

Just as a broadened theory provides a framework for thinking through those motivations that we work with every day in the psychoanalytic situation, it also provides a broadened and clarified view of multiple function. When Waelder (1936) described this, he emphasized that every behavior had functions (to varying degrees) with regard to drive gratification, adaptation, conscience, and repetition. As I read his work, repetition was never really clear. Was this the operation of Freud's (1920) abstract notion of a repetition compulsion as an expression of a death instinct? Or was it some variant of the child's repeatedly throwing the spool out of the crib, mastering goodbye and return? Today it can be clarified in terms of the tendency to repeat old object relationships, a repetition powered by the pleasure and the strain trauma in those relationships, as just described. Additionally, the functions of every behavior can be enlarged to include the function of the maintenance of self-esteem, continuity, cohesion, or boundaries (or its negative forms, when those are what are self-defining). In this way we include more richly and more accurately what we may find and interpret in any of the patient's productions.

A broadened theory has a home for a broadened understanding of development, starting with the "infantile danger situations" (Freud, 1926). Loss of the object can now be seen to reflect both the need for the object of drive satisfaction and the attachment to the primary caretaker per se. Feared loss of the love of the object seems now to reflect displaced forms of a drive-based wish for the object, continued direct expression of core attachment needs, and the object's love as the source and reflector of both self-esteem and, at times, the very sense of self. Loss of bodily integrity (and castration) as well as loss of superego approval remain core danger situations. But I would add to the list loss of sense of self, reflecting the continuity of both the inner subjective state and the characteristic defensive style. Fear of the strange, fear of overwhelming affect, and Anna Freud's (1936) "fear of the strength of the instincts" (which would obliterate the nascent self) are also relevant here.

Finally, a broadened theory expands (to the spheres of drive, ego, object, and self) our understanding of the developmental "organizers" in Spitz's (1965) sense—that is, normal developmental steps that reflect fairly sharp shifts in function, seen both as reflecting the joining together of past developmental achievements and, once emerged, as changing individual function ever after. The three organizers that Spitz identified were the nonspecific smile, the eight-months stranger anxiety, and the emergence of the "no." Going on from there, and in like spirit, the psychic representation of bodily urge or the first sublimation of such an urge may be seen as one such organizer in the drive sphere, as is, for example, the internalization of regulatory mechanisms (in contrast to reliance on caretakers) in the ego sphere, or the recognition and evolution of specific expectancies regarding the primary caretaker in the object relational sphere, or the emergence of self-other differentiation and the sense of "I" in the self sphere.

The overall point is that a broadened general theory translates also into enrichment of our understanding of motivation, multiple function, infantile danger situations, developmental organizers, and, potentially, all aspects of theory. And these part-theories are the groundwork for understanding the diverse presentations that we hear about in our clinical work.

Concluding Remarks

Metaphorically the psychoanalytic view of the mind is that of a deep well—deep in that its formative sources are from long ago and its current workings are largely unconscious. But the well of the mind is as wide as it is deep—wide enough to contain the array of motives, mental contents, and mechanisms that diverse analysts have described. Within this deep well of the mind, unconscious or marginally conscious drive, ego, object relational, and self phenomena all interplay. And the ego, to continue the metaphor, serves as the plumbing for the well. It is like a set of valves determining which unconscious forces will be shut off or released and deflecting release in this direction or that. Ego function, in this conception, is equally relevant to issues of drive, object relations, self, and unconscious ego itself.

I have tried to present the expansion of psychoanalytic theories as reflective of organic growth, on the basis of cultural history, the demands of the theory itself, new modes of observation, and, in particular, our position in evolution. I have then given three bases for the integration of these diverse conceptions (developmentally in the child, hierarchically in the formed adult, and clinically in our work with patients). I have also reviewed three major critiques of the approach (eclecticism, the question of the extricability of concepts from the larger theories in which they have been lodged, and the danger of clinical arbitrariness) and have attempted to respond to these critiques. Finally, I have suggested some of the clinical and theoretical gains from this expanded view.

The view presented here can be seen to provide alternative modes of telling the patient's story—a "coherence" (Hanly, 1990) or hermeneutic view. My own leaning is, however, to see it (again using Hanly's word) in "correspondence" terms—that is, more closely corresponding to the actual development and functioning of mind. These multiple modes of description of mental life represent the reality "out there," even though it is a reality (and a history) never fully knowable. In my experience interpretation of these various aspects of mind reaches the patient, matching ongoing experience as the patient feels it to be. In this manner, the broadening of theory productively underlies the growth of diversity in technique.

Part II Direction in Psychoanalytic Technique

Having described the current diversity in psychoanalytic theory and some of the sources of a parallel diversity in technique, I intend in this section to consider specific details within the broad domain of psychoanalytic technique. In no way are my remarks here a general theory of technique; to attempt that would be inconsistent with what I have outlined thus far. Instead, I provide details, the complex considerations that support our general ways of working and our specific modes of intervention in a given clinical instance. What I give are building blocks—building blocks not for a general theory, but, rather, for the working clinician to use in thinking about the clinical enterprise as he or she conducts it daily and to use in creating the possibility for intervention.

Contributions to a theory of technique for psychoanalysis have had changing foci over the decades. Following his earliest focus on the recovery of traumatic memories Freud shifted to making unconscious fantasies conscious or, in the language of the later structural theory, to bringing ego control to areas previously under the domination of the id. The statement "Where id was there shall ego be" (Freud, 1933) includes reference to the ego, but is still very much tied to Freud's earliest theories of technique and the effort to reach and make conscious what is pathogenic and unknown. But later, ego psychology made additional impacts on the theory of technique with its attention to the analytic surface, to defense and character, to adaptation and the conflict-free sphere, and to anxiety as a signal of danger, among other things. Another trend, originating in the years of the development of ego psychology but reaching its crescendo only in more recent decades, was a focus on the analysis of transference (Gill, 1982)—a focus so strong that it led to a lesser but still important counterfocus on the role of extratransference interpretation. The proliferation of near-alternative theories of mind within psychoanalysis, most notably object relations theories and self psychology, also reverberated through the theory of technique, with implications for how mind is conceived of, how its workings are communicated to the patient, and how the conception of mind affects the analyst's mode of intervention. The burgeoning of infant research, adding to the growth of child analysis, created a surge of writings on the implications of developmental theory for technique. Most recently, discussions of technique have centered on the here-and-now, between-two-persons events of the session, conceptualized variously in terms of intersubjectivity, constructivism, a two-person (by contrast to a one-person) psychology of the analytic situation, and transference-countertransference enactments.

All the technical considerations I have just listed are treated, more or less extensively, in the following chapters. For the individual committed to any single approach, each of my discussions will seem too scant. And if my aim were to do full justice to any one of them, my discussions would indeed be insufficient. My aim instead is to work from the position that everything we have learned regarding technique is still relevant today. I try to walk among the parts, clarifying, contrasting, emphasizing, and balancing wherever I can and whenever I see a gain in so doing.

My essential rationale for this approach is straightforward enough. The patient has unconscious fantasies, intrapsychic conflict, a functioning conscience, and a capacity for ego function, all of which deserve our attention. The patient has a developmental history but also has a contemporary life, including the immediate life within the session, all of which deserve our attention. The person who comes to analysis also has an intrapsychic life that is carried around inside but is then expressed in the two-person situation of the analysis, and both the life "carried inside" and the two-person expressions of it deserve our attention. Our attention is given not in an arbitrary or equalizing way but according to where the patient seems to be at on that day, varying for different patients, different days, different points in the analysis. This of course is subject to multiple readings, so we have no choice but to do our best to listen and understand. I believe we will do better if we keep the multitude of possibilities in mind.

In Chapter 3, I try to locate and describe some of the multiple modes of therapeutic action in the highly individualized process of psychoanalysis. My focus is on some of the many permutations and combinations of interpretive and relational effects and the opportunities and limitations they involve. Chapter 4 follows up on these ideas by looking at relational effects operative at the core of the interpretive process itself.

In Chapter 5 I start from a different perspective, examining the place of the ego in the clinical process, endeavoring to show the ego in its living clinical reality rather than in its metapsychological dress. In Chapter 6, I examine phenomena of defect, deficit, and conflict, which require object relational and ego psychological understandings in the course of interpretive and relational work with them.

Chapter 7 returns to the theme of Chapter 2. In it, I try to show the clinical reasoning entering into the choice of interpretation within and between the several different psychoanalytic psychologies—drive, ego, object, and self. Chapter 8 addresses developmental considerations as they enter into adult psychoanalytic or psychotherapeutic work.

These chapters express my belief that there is a great diversity in current psychoanalytic ways of working, but it is not random. There is much we know and much we can think about. I give some thoughts on a few of the details.

3 Therapeutic Actions of Psychoanalysis: The Mix of Interpretation and Relationship

The title of this chapter follows from Strachey's (1934) and Loewald's (1960) papers on therapeutic action (except for the change to plural, therapeutic *actions*). Kohut (1984) used the more engaging title "How Does Analysis Cure?" for his treatment of this same subject. Each author approached the subject from his own conceptual vantage point, and I do the same. My vantage point is twofold: first, where I am now as an analyst, how my work has evolved and is evolving; and second, where the field of psychoanalysis is now, with all its intellectual multiplicity, uncertainty, and potentiality. The question of therapeutic action—in particular in its multiple forms and with special attention to interpretive and relational aspects—is an appropriate place to begin this discussion of directions within the diversity of psychoanalytic technique.

All the published views regarding therapeutic action—that is, how the process works to bring about change—essentially address variants on two components: understanding (and the associated interpretive activity) and the relationship (viewed in many different ways). Each can be approached independently to a degree but more often they are seen as intertwined. The intertwining takes a variety of forms, and that will be the thrust of the second, and larger, part of this chapter. Before discussing multiplicity, however, I want to address the highly individualized nature of the therapeutic impact, which is individualized in terms of both patient and analyst, though still of necessity involving the intertwined domains of understanding and the relationship. I begin with the individualized nature of the process.

Freud (1900) saw dreams as the "royal road to a knowledge of the unconscious." In his technical writings, however, he was careful not to give dreams pride of place. They were not necessarily to be pursued until fully understood; rather, the analyst was to follow the patient's associations and be ready to shift the domain of the work within the session and in the next session. But the "royal road" metaphor did convey the idea that "the unconscious" was the place to get to, and certainly dreams were seen as a good way, the best way, to get there. Therapeutic action presumably required getting to the unconscious via one road or another. But gradually, with the development of ego psychology, defense and character structure became equally important places to get to. They too could be unconscious, but generally not in exactly the same form as unconscious fantasies or wishes. And they could be ego-syntonic aspects of ordinary functioning toward which the patient had to be helped to develop a more introspective and questioning attitude. Still later, with reference either to unconscious fantasy and wish or to character and defense, transference and, later, transference-countertransference engagements in the here-and-now began to seem to be more of a royal road. Then there is the argument that we should not be on any road, royal or otherwise, going anywhere—but rather should be staying in as close touch as possible with the patient's current psychic reality.

Today's psychoanalytic climate suggests that not only which road to follow but also where we want to go (if anywhere) varies with the individual patient, even the individual session. Only that is a fully psychoanalytic view. We cannot know in advance which road will be best for a particular territory at a particular time (that is, a given patient's mind now): *that* we discover in each analysis and, to a degree, in each session. It is discovered, or created, by and within the analytic pair. So the answer to the question, What is the therapeutic action of psychoanalysis? includes more questions: For whom? (that is, which patient) At what time? (that is, now). The answer also includes asking, In whose hands? (which analyst). Partly by training, but deeply by character and history, we analysts each bring into our work differential sensitivities, not only to this or that content (fantasies, object relations, affects) but also to the domains in which the work can happen—past, outside present, transference, countertransference, here-and-now. Our "third ears" in analysis have differential attunements, and we hope that this ear is not deaf in any region.

We bring our own personalities into the work, despite the place of relative anonymity as one of the legs of the tripod on which analysis stands (that is, anonymity, neutrality, and abstinence). My self-understanding, for example, is that (among those characteristics that I am willing to discuss here) a seriousness, even earnestness, of style and purpose, a deeply developmental point of view, and an open, perhaps at times experimental, stance pervade my analytic style; each of these aspects, however, has a history of conflict and conflict resolution, and each of them sits comfortably now within the setting of what I regard as my analytic work ego. I presume it is the same for each of us. Were we a fly on the wall in any particular analyst's office, we would see highly individualized ways of working that reflect personal style. And even more, were we a fly inside the head of the analyst, or could we stop the analytic action and have the analyst explore (through free association or self-examination) his or her intervention choices, we would uncover much about a blend of technical responsivity and choice, on the one hand, and about varyingly transformed character, conflict, and history, on the other. (See Grossman, 1996, for an example of this self-examination.) A certain amount of the personal side of my analytic work will be included here; it is one of the ways we learn from each other.

Thus, the therapeutic action of psychoanalysis is subtly and deeply individualized through the features of both the patient and the analyst. However, this need not lead to either a nihilistic or a solipsistic point of view. Where we do not naturally fly we can at least learn to walk. And no patient is totally unidimensional in what he or she can draw from or work with. Progress is made on dirt paths, too, even in the absence of royal superhighways.

There is a considerable area where communication is possible. Few of us today are blind to the possibilities of thinking in the conceptual-developmental terms of drives (or urges or impulses), of ego functions (like defense, reality testing, and adaptation), of object relations (both internal and extenal), and of the loose collection of phenomena referred to as "self" (such as esteem, wholeness and continuity, boundaries, and agency). Most of us are aware that the technical domains of work in the past life, the outside present life, the transference, the here-and-now transference, the transference-countertransference interaction, and work with a one-person or a two-person psychology are all on the theory-of-technique table currently. We sometimes even think we have consensus within these broad categories.

Having in mind the general areas in which active communication does take place in the literature and in discussions, I treat a few of the intertwinings of understanding and the patient-analyst relationship that go into the therapeutic action of an analysis. But having in mind also the endlessly varied and highly individualized nature of the process, I am unable to give more than a few isolated ideas relevant to the topic. I draw on observations from my own work recently. I speak briefly on four subjects: understanding in itself, supposedly outside of the transference; the relationship in itself, with reference to its so-called nonspecific effects; understanding in the relationship—that is, the various aspects of transference; and the two-person psychology of the analytic situation, with particular reference to self-disclosure.

Four Commentaries

I use the plural, therapeutic *actions*, in my chapter title. In an era of explosive growth in psychoanalysis—of concepts of how mind is organized, of what happens within and between the two members of the analytic pair in a session, and of the range of patients for whom psychoanalysis is used—it is neither wise nor useful to think in terms of searching out a single effective therapeutic agent.

Understanding in Itself

Understanding in itself is supposedly "outside the transference." A few years ago, under the sway of what I thought was my clinical experience and also, probably, of tides in the literature, I found myself heavily emphasizing transference interpretation in my surpervision and clinical teaching. But slowly I discovered that my own clinical work was more balanced than what I had been teaching. It may be that work in the transference has a powerful pull on the analyst, which exaggerates its centrality. This is by no means meant to diminish the significance of work in the transference but rather to elevate work that happens to be focused on the outside life, the remembered life, or the constructed life. I now believe that this more fairly represents my own clinical observations. There are three aspects to why this is so.

First, no work is every completely "outside the transference." Even when the you-and-me, the here-and-now, does not enter into the content, the work is taking place in the context of a significant and usually intense relationship, within a significant and usually intense process. It may not be *about* the transference, but it takes place in the transference setting, and there is plenty of affect in both the content and the setting. This work is not affectively bland, and if it is, *that* is something to be understood.

Second, work in the transference has its impact not only because it is immediately visible in the present (if it is thus visible) but because it is where the heat is, and optimal heat seems to generate significant work. But for all patients at times, for some even most of the time, the heat will be elsewhere—for example, in the remembered past, in a current outside relationship, in the anguished self-recognition of the limitations and pain imposed by character. At such times, transference interpretation may be canned heat and miss the real action, or something about the patient's relatedness or character may make transference work difficult to reach.

Third, evolution gave humans a large forebrain capable of producing miraculous things. Neither the intensity and immediacy of work in the transference nor the immense and pervasive significance of relationships should blind us to the power of cognitive understanding. It can reveal wishes and irrational beliefs and transferred object relations in the outside life, it can produce an organized perspective on personal history, and it can order, reorganize, and add to work that has been accomplished in other (say, transference) domains, increasing the patient's hold on the material.

Let me make two other specific points about understandings reached—not, I would now say, "outside the transference," for nothing is outside of it—but not about the transference. The first entails work with dreams. My way of working with them remains fairly traditional (though I have no unified theory of dream formation, and I may interpret from numerous points of view). With many, but not all, patients I find this work invaluable. While the patient's associations may lead clearly to transference themes, and the meanings are often constructed between us, the associative process is usually experienced as very much the patient's own thoughts, often leading to internal dynamic understandings or to the new significance of memories quite aside from transference. Since the dream is experienced as being entirely the patient's own cognitive product and mystifying at the surface, understanding produced here can be experienced with conviction.

I also want to mention the significance of the use of words. Here I draw on Loewald's (1960) paper on therapeutic action, though without adding to it. Both the analyst's use of words and the patient's use of words to "reach the analyst"—sometimes, for the patient, putting a specific inner experience into words for the first time—permit inchoate inner experience to become thinkable, sayable. This itself is a significant part of the therapeutic action, being both a part of understanding and the beginning of the possibility of further understanding as thoughts come into being through words. Similarly, Katan (1961) wrote of the significance of the naming of affects by the developing child's mother. These two papers reflect part of the developmental work of an analysis. This use of words could be thought of as one of the so-called nonspecific effects of the analytic relationship. But, provided that the words are translations of the inchoate, of the unspoken and unthinkable, it is truly an analytic effect, inescapably embedded in the analytic relationship and process.

The So-Called Nonspecific Effects

This last point serves as a transition to the domain of the relationship in itself and the so-called nonspecific factors in the therapeutic action of psychoanalysis. The nonspecific factors that I now address are those represented in the analyst's reliability, putting the patient's interests first, and offering full attention and nonjudgmental listening, among other things. They are what Alexander referred to when he spoke of corrective emotional experience—not that part of his discussion (Alexander, 1956) in which he recommended deciding what the patient needed and somehow playacting the part, but rather his statement that the analyst *is* different from the parents-of-childhood, and that this is indispensable for the work (Alexander, 1948). It is the "holding" background of the relationship, in Winnicott's (1965) term—not necessarily in the sense that it re-creates a safe childhood (which, may never have existed) but in the sense that it provides a current context of safety within which the patient can explore inner life, dare to address issues here-and-now in the analytic relationthip, and further risk personal change.

But, alas, nothing is simple in analysis. We all see the world through different colored glasses; thus the patient may not feel the supposed safety of the relationship. This or that "nonspecific factor" supposedly contributing to productive therapeutic action can instead be experienced as exposing, depriving, demanding, controlling, seducing, or judging, to name only a few possible experiences.

Development in the child and change in the analysand take place best in the context of support and challenge. For the growing child, this means a holding environment and expectations and opportunities for growth. In psychoanalysis, the challenge part comes from interpretation and from the free-association process itself. The support part comes from these so-called nonspecific factors (though ultimately, perhaps even more from the fact of understanding oneself). But, and here is my point, for some patients and in some areas, the possibility of making use of reliability, attentive listening, nonjudgmentalness, and the placing of the analyst's personal needs in the background—the possibility of making use of these is itself an *achievement* of the analysis, coming about only after various dynamically based interferences are sorted out and understood. In the next chapter, in which I analyze an aspect of the psychoanalytic process, I try to show that these background relationship factors often have their maximal impact at the moment of interpretation. I shall not anticipate that whole chapter here, but it follows the lines of Strachey's (1934) discussion of the mutative power of transference interpretation, in that instance (as seen by Strachey) because the experience of the analyst's nonjudgmentalness simultaneously with and in contrast to the analyst's interpretation of the patient's view of him or her as a punitive conscience is precisely what makes for change. For the patient to be able to experience the analyst as nonjudgmental, however, considerable analytic work is often required.

So much (though briefly) for dynamic interferences with the patient's capacity to draw beneficially on the relational context. There are also "traumatic" interferences, discussed more fully in Chapter 6. I am referring to ways in which the ordinary analytic situation as it is customarily carried out—independent now, for discussion's sake, of any pathology in the analyst—can be traumatizing for a particular patient, or retraumatizing because it repeats (as the patient experiences it) some past trauma in the relation to (usually) a parent. Ordinarily this is a "strain trauma" (Kris, 1956), some repetitive mishandling by a parent that becomes traumatic only cumulatively. In the reverse, some aspect of the ordinary analytic setup can be powerfully ameliorative for a patient because it reverses such strain trauma. In both instances (traumatizing or ameliorative), what would be a background factor in the relationship may rise to focal awareness and intensity and can itself be the subject of analytic work, or sometimes, in the case of traumatizing aspects of the setup, the subject of alteration of the analytic setup. At this point I will indicate briefly what I mean but reserve further discussion for Chapter 6.

As for the ameliorative aspect, I think of a patient for whom my reliable presence (that is, not arriving late, never missing a session except with advance notification) played a significant role. This reliability seemed to me ordinary analytic behavior, part of the analytic contract. As such it could be seen as part of the nonspecific background that (potentially) affects a patient positively. But with this patient, it was not "nonspecific" at all. Because of her history, this otherwise background factor achieved primary importance. Loss and separation had been issues throughout her life, but only late in the work did reliability-as-nonloss achieve verbalization between us.

More problematic and probably more dramatic are those instances where ordinary analytic behavior is retraumatizing. I think of instances where silences—to me, no more than ordinary ones, but not so for the patient—were disorganizing or reproduced intolerable object loss, and of other instances where interpretations produced feelings of being controlled. Each of these scenarios repeated aspects of the patient's history-as-experienced. I wish to make three points about these phenomena: (1) they were extremely powerful in their negative effects, producing rage and disorganization; (2) while they were talked about, sometimes profitably, they also required changes in the way I worked—that is, in the behavior experienced as retraumatizing; and (3) having become aware of the phenomenon, I now find that I am more capable of becoming aware of it again, and do so in surprising places. I ask myself how I did analysis before I was sensitized to these issues, because they are significant parts of the analysis. In addition to the importance of recognizing what was going on, and making the sometimes necessary technical alterations in response, is the importance of working on the place of these experiences in the patient's life, exploring the (usually well-remembered) history, and analyzing the fantasies that have developed around the strain trauma.

This concludes my brief remarks on the relationship factors in themselves, the so-called nonspecific factors, which can turn out not to be so nonspecific after all. Next is the topic of understandings in the relationship—that is, transference interpretations. How is what I have been describing different from work in the transference as traditionally conceived? In a way, the retraumatizing effects are to transference analysis what the so-called actual neuroses were to the neuroses per se for Freud. That is, I see the retraumatizing effects as "real" (in some quantity-of-immediate-impact terms, and because of aspects of the particular life history) and not simply subject to alteration via interpretation; Kohut's (1977, 1984) work contributes to much of this point of view. Description and reconstruction of origins have an important place in relation to these strain trauma and their repetition in the analysis, but not yet interpretation in the here-and-now. The more usual transference analysis can more readily be approached directly with interpretation.

A Few Notes on Transference

I turn now to understandings in the relationship, transference analysis (although it is clear that I have just softened the distinction between this and the so-called nonspecific factors). Transference is still an evolving and expanding concept. Originally transference interpretation took the form (schematically), "You think you are talking about me but you are really talking about someone else back then or out there." Then it began to be altered or added to, taking the form, "You think you are talking about someone out there, but you are really talking about me" (or about us). I believe this subsumes what Merton Gill (1982) referred to as analysis of resistance to awareness of the transference—that is, widening the analysand's awareness of transference. More recently, transference has also come to refer to whatever is happening here-and-now, in the office, between analyst and analysand (which may be quite separate from whatever the patient happens to be saying). It may focus on the mood created in the office, the form of self-presentation, the use the patient is making of the analyst, and the like. Additionally there is the transference work that occurs with some patients who regularly and explicitly talk about the analyst and their relation to him or her. These are patients who might seem to the uninitiated to be curable by leaving the analysis; all their problems seem to be with the analyst or the analysis. The analyst works with this form of the here-and-now presumably with the underlying idea that the analytic events are a microcosm of the patient's world and that therefore the work can be properly done within the analysis. This is all powerful stuff analytically speaking, and I can easily subscribe to the view that it is often the center of the analytic work—though certainly not *necessarily*. Work in the transference can have an immediacy that makes it affectively powerful and a visibility and clarity that make it real—both affectivity and realness increasing the therapeutic impact of the work. But this immediacy and affectivity can also translate into a pull on the analyst for work in the transference; one has to be cautious with respect to distinguishing between work that is for the analyst and work that is for the patient.

Work in the transference, like any aspect of technique, has its dangers if it is too driven by ideology (that is, theory) or by the requirements of the analyst's character and need-system. Interpretations in the transference often have the greatest heat, and analytic interpretation is best offered in a reasonably warm to hot atmosphere: not too cold and not so hot as to be unusable. So sometimes we move out of the transference to reduce the heat ("You are really talking about someone else"). But again we have to be sure who—the patient or the analyst—either cannot stand the heat or requires the heat of the "between us" work. Then there is the statement, "You think you are talking about someone else but you are really talking about me" (or you and me, or here). Undoubtedly, this form of transference interpretation is a powerful tool when properly used, but readily subject to knee-jerk usage by the analyst, making it, like any reflex, entirely predictable. I have seen this too frequently in supervisory experiences in recent years. It is even more problematic when it stems from sources deeply rooted in the personality of the analyst, reflecting self-absorption or some requirement of the analyst's personality to matter, to be powerful, to feel loved, or to feel alive. The interpretation and understanding of what is going on in the office, between us, right now, is also an extraordinarily powerful tool, but carries the danger of a kind of shared solipsism unless the work moves back and forth between the here-and-now, the outside life, and the past.

The gains in the analyst's being able to work in any of the transference domains just listed, but additionally in dreams, in the reconstructed past, or in the current life are clear. It is vital to be able to work where the patient is (where the psychological heat is) at any given moment and thus truly work in the region of immediacy, yet also retain a capacity for surprise, for the novel, as the patient is viewed now through one lens, now through another, keeping our minds open to countless possibilities just as we work toward increased awareness in the analysand's mind. But the personal factor enters in heavily. On the one hand, the analyst's commitment to a particular domain of the work (transferential, interactive, intersubjective, reconstructive, "deep" in the mind) may be characterologically driven or (in its more public aspect) driven by group loyalty or devotion to authority—all readily explained as a theory of technique. I know that phenomenon in myself, where a balanced, multiperspective view in theory and technique has deep characterological sources and also involves a devotion to particular formative ego ideal figures. My only hope can be that the view I espouse draws on but is not controlled by such sources. On the other hand, as I noted earlier, we have to recognize that each of us has a differential sensitivity to, or capacity for, this or that way of working.

The Two-Person Psychology and Self-Disclosure

The countertransference concept has undergone an evolution similar to the transference concept. It now includes all of the following: "I am feeling or thinking something, and though it may be stimulated by our current work it is about me; it is for me to work on." Then we move to: "I am feeling or thinking something and it is stimulated by you, the person you are, and if I process it I can learn about you from it; it is indeed about you." Next is: "Something is happening between us here and I think I have been caught up in it and detect it in my way of working; if I can process it and put it into words, we will learn something about you."

Since my way of interpreting often includes some reference to the evidence on which it is based, drawing on evidence in my subjective or automatic behavioral reactions to a particular patient has led me to the issue of the two-person psychology of the analytic situation and in turn to the issue of self-disclosure. But this is not the only route that takes me there. For I assume that most of us are aware by now of the "two-personness" of the analytic situation, of the analyst's role in eliciting and shaping the material, not only by his or her interpretations, but by ways of thinking that are experienced as automatic and even "impersonal" (that is, not self-revealing or influence-carrying) and also by the analyst's style and presence in the office. I take it for granted that the analyst has to become aware of these effects in this particular analysis now, just as he or she becomes aware of anything else. The only real question for me is whether any of this should be made explicit, and, if so, how and when and what. The difference I see—and it is probably not absolute—is between understanding the patient as he or she is seen in relation to me, and understanding us both as we interact together here-and-now. The understandings of me that enter in are, so far as I know (and I am aware of questions about who is or is not the expert on reality), understandings of me in the interaction with this particular patient—that is, potentially informing us of something about the patient. These, too, by their very nature, combine understanding and relationship factors, my theme here.

Before proceeding, I interject one note. In the choice between slippery slope and conceptual inconsistency in this area, I stand with the latter. In my observation of my own work, I do not find myself going down the slope from recognition of the two-person psychology to the idea that everything lies in that domain. Perhaps there always is a second person affecting things, either in actuality or in the mind. Nonetheless I find, for good or ill, that most of what I offer to the patient, and even most of how I hear the patient, is about the one-person psychology of the patient's intrapsychic world (including transference routes into this, of course). My ultimate anchor is my inner sense of having an intrapsychic world that I carry with me into each new situation; I assume it is the same for the patient. My psychoanalytic history, as student and then practitioner, has contributed to this anchoring. My choice of the one-person view does involve a conceptual inconsistency, however. At the level of a theory of mind and its operation, I recognize the two-personness of the analytic situation; but on the level of clinical intervention, a one-person view often seems most valuable.

Self-disclosure in an analysis, however modest, is not part of my psychoanalytic pedigree and has entered only slowly into my work. My approach to it has been cautious and watchful, and my experience with it, though limited, has been good (in my judgment). My entry into this arena is, again, a reflection of the personal and of the issues alive in the field today. For some readers, my examples will seem hardly novel and merely evidence that I am finally catching on; I share those attitudes somewhat. My point is that we each have ways of working that reflect professional history and personal issues, and this cautious approach to self-disclosure reflects my own.

As I try, for present purposes, to describe how self-disclosure came to seem a fairly natural step, one at least worth trying, I think of several things. First, I have had (as I am sure is common) experiences with particular patients who read me remarkably well. Sometimes in my character, sometimes in my depths, what I thought was "anonymous" seems to be thoroughly part of the session, though I neither confirm nor disconfirm the patient's readings. And this view of me (in the patient) was something we worked on and with. Self-disclosure must already have occurred implicitly rather than through words with explicit intent to disclose. Second, I have had some clinical experiences in which my confirmation of the patient's reality sense—particularly in areas of some form of abuse surrounded by parental hypocrisy and denial—seemed to play an extremely significant and beneficial role at a certain point in the analysis. I, too, am part of the patient's reality. Sometimes it has seemed evasive, if not hypocritical and denying (like the family), to sidestep that fact. Third, questions about the analyst's authority—about who is the expert on reality anyway—narrow the divide between patient and analyst. While I renounce neither my expertise with regard to mental functioning nor the requirement that I aspire to such expertise, the narrowing of the divide has been a democratizing factor in the work that has probably facilitated my utilizing self-disclosure at times. Fourth, I have been aware for a while now that one's theory of technique, even, say, the value of free association (Aron, 1990; Ogden, 1996), is tied to one's theory of mind and of therapeutic action. If the therapeutic action is seen as related to patient-analyst interaction, free association can come to be seen as much less central. This is not the predominant view with which I work, but my awareness of compelling questions about the relation between technique and change, and between theory of technique and theory of mind, provides an intellectual context for exploring the new, or what is new for any particular individual. And, finally, significant discussions of self-disclosure in the literature—for example, in Bollas's (1983) paper on expressive use of the countertransference or in Renik's work (1995)—also lie in the intellectual background for me.

I turn now to three situations, all involving self-disclosure about the "me" who appears in the analytic work with this patient now. In each instance, though for different reasons, I thought it was potentially valuable to bring my subjectivity explicitly into the work. For reasons of confidentiality, I am fairly sketchy in each description.

My first example is one that came up in parallel form with two different patients. In each instance, the patient was hesitantly struggling to become aware of something disturbing about him or herself. In each case we were well into the analysis, and we had considerable analytic work behind us. One patient was becoming aware of an emotional distance between himself and others; the other, of what was felt to be a dangerously destructive form of anger, one that would imperil others and her relationships to them. In each instance, my experience was the same: I knew what they were referring to, and I could only then, through the patient's insight, fully articulate to myself that I had been responding to these features all along, that each had affected my way of working with the patient. Given the intimacy and trust in those analytic relationships, and given both patients' struggle to find words for these inner experiences, I felt that the strongest confirmation I could give to each, at the same time offering an opportunity to see its impact on others and to go through the experience firsthand, was to confirm it through my own observation about its impact on my way of working with them. Until then I had not fully articulated to myself this variation in my work style and even less its role in what lay waiting to be understood about the patients. Their dawning self-understanding enhanced my understanding—in one instance of a hesitance to "intrude" on the patient (the one who became aware of setting up an emotional distance) and in the other a caution about triggering anger. My self-disclosure of how I had been sensing these features in them and how that had affected my way of working with them was indeed confirming. In the instance of the emotional distance, it had the immediate paradoxical effect of promoting intimacy: for the patient it meant that we understood together. This was only the beginning of what became extensive analytic work. In the other case, the outcome was stormier, for my hesitance in the face of her anger at first confirmed for her the true dangerousness of that anger. This became the focus of the work for quite some time; the outcome seemed to me highly productive, precisely because of the sense that we were in this together, bearing the danger of the anger and managing to continue. I doubt that the work could have been as powerful in the process and productive in the outcome had I not self-disclosed, though there is no way to know that for certain.

My second pair of examples again has a commonality in form: In both I was in a dilemma about how to communicate productively, or, more accurately, I was in what I felt could become a destructive stalemate. I chose, in slightly different ways in the two instances, to focus on my sense of dilemma. In the first patient, a misunderstanding occurred in our communication. I thought I understood something he said, but he disconfirmed my understanding. Similarly, the patient had had the experience of understanding what I had said in a way that I thought was miles from what I intended. Both of us experienced a wide gap in being understood. These kinds of misunderstandings played a significant and destructive role in his contemporary everyday object relations. I believed that numerous unsuccessful and (for the patient) irritating attempts had been made to deal with them as features of the patient in treatments prior to our own; I had heard much about them. I chose at this point to explore the in-office event between us as a way of analyzing the patient. The patient's effect on me, my experience of being misunderstood and of the gap between my intended and received meaning, and my surprise at the gap in my understanding of the patient all became part of the work. I felt I seized a present in-the-office opportunity; I just happened to be part of the experience and part of what was to be explored. This did not include self-analysis with the patient, only disclosure and focal exploration of my experience of and with the patient. I brought in my subjectivity, not my self-analysis. What seemed to happen through my self-disclosure was that the misunderstanding lost its power as a destructive event in which we were ensnared and became an event that we could observe together.

The other instance of this kind involved a patient who seemed to go into psychological crisis in response to several things I said, remarks that he could take as a moralistic judgment, on the one hand, or as a seduction, a giving of license, on the other. We had been through these crises more than once, and, while this dilemma is not rare in an analysis, his responses were marked by serious disruptions of his functioning in ordinary life and by gross ruptures in the relationship between us. When I tried to point out something about his response—dynamically, or even just descriptively—that itself became a judgment or a seduction, condemning something in him or opening it up for free expression. I had at times gotten caught up in the attempt to skirt the problem by finding a "right" response, but these responses turned out to be so vague or empty that they dissolved into the air. But now, for whatever reason, I found myself able to turn to an examination of the process itself. I offered the patient my subjective experience of the dilemma and described interventions I found myself considering but uncertain about; I described my sense of what I felt was the danger in each response I might make. What I said had the effect of making the whole process—the patient's impact on me, mine on the patient, and my *potential* interventions (which were given as inner thoughts rather than as actual statements to the patient)—an object for analysis between us rather than a specific action or failed action by me on the patient. That step of once-removal, which in this instance involved my disclosing my subjective dilemma (reflected in my doubts about each of my possible responses), enabled the work to proceed.

The third example where I brought self-disclosure into the work was my first self-conscious experience with it, quite a few years ago, before "self-disclosure" was even part of my psychoanalytic vocabulary. My experience was that I was simply doing what I felt was necessary to do in the work. It occurred with a man from whom I had always experienced a powerful pull for his knowing my internal world, and in particular his place in it. What I thought was good work in the analysis over time eventually convinced me that this was the point around which much of his psychic life, psychic pain, and developmental history were organized. That is, his place in the inner object world of the other was never well defined. His inner life and fantasies seemed to build heavily on a history with a physically present but psychically grossly absent mother throughout his infancy and childhood, so far as could be determined. We eventually did considerable work on this, both about how it operated in the present and about its sources in the past. But ultimately I came to believe that there were significant traumatic and deficit features in the history that underlay his presenting problems in this area, and that it would be useful for the work for him to have some awareness that he *had* an existence in my inner life. Many remarks I might have made about that fact seemed trivial or condescending. I asked myself what I could say that would not be alien to the process in which we were engaged—the process, that is, of analyzing this very phenomenon. What I finally chose to say was something about my experience of the pull for knowledge of my inner life that came from him, and how I had wondered about it and come to understand it in relation to his uncertainty about whether he existed there; that is, I spoke of his place in my inner life with regard to the very issue we were working on. It was that part of him that he wanted to be sure I had registered inside. The circle was complete, the elements fit together, and the analysis—including the analysis of this phenomenon—proceeded.

Self-disclosure of the perhaps modest, perhaps not so modest, sorts I have been describing seem a bit like the discovery of speaking prose. It is not that I have been doing it all my life, but it does not seem all that far from what I have been doing. I have already referred to Sandler's (1981) description of the "intellectual contortions" (p. 187) that theoreticians of a certain era went through to manage to express all psychoanalytic discoveries in drive-defense terms. In a related way—that is, driven by inner introjects and commands—I think of the contortions I have gone through with patients so as not to reveal anything about my inner life. Complete secrecy is not possible in any case, and the opposite, cautiously approached, can be useful.

Concluding Remarks

I have touched briefly on a few characteristics of the problem of therapeutic action, in each instance addressing an aspect of the interweaving of understanding and relationship. In the case of understandings supposedly outside the transference, I have tried both to highlight their value in themselves and to show that, in any event, they are embedded in the whole analytic relationship and process. They take place in the transference though they are not about the transference. In the case of the so-called nonspecific factors in the analytic relationship, I have tried to show that they may in fact be quite specific and may become focal for certain patients, depending on individual history and dynamics, and require considerable personalized understanding. In the case of transference analysis, which I described in its several aspects and take to be central in the work, I chose to be cautious and to point out a few potential problems and excesses in its use. And in the case of the two-person psychology of the analysis I chose to discuss my explorations in the domain of self-disclosure, emphasizing understanding of events in the patient-analyst relationship.

I have allowed myself this unsystematic and particularizing approach because I believe, aside from our general agreement that the therapeutic action of psychoanalysis derives from various intertwinings of understanding and of the patient-analyst relationship, that the actuality of therapeutic impact is endlessly variable—dependent on features of the patient, the analyst, and the pair—and so a consideration of one particular person's recent thoughts and experiences gives at least a glance into the analytic setting.

Our reports on analytic work are sharply limited by issues of patient confidentiality. But they are also obviously limited by the analyst's sense of personal privacy. Within the sense of my own privacy, I have tried to depict aspects of the analytic process as I currently struggle with it. In the next chapter, I examine the particularly significant mix of interpretive and relationship effects that occurs in certain instances precisely at the moment of interpretation.

4 A Contribution to the Analysis of the Psychoanalytic Process

In a series of papers on the psychoanalytic process published in the *Psychoanalytic Quarterly* in 1990, one of the major issues involved the question of how we are to conceive of the two-person interactional features inherently present in a psychoanalysis and the impact of this feature on our understanding of the core psychoanalytic process. In his own contribution to that discussion, Compton (1990) wrote: "Once the role of the analyst as participant observer (like that of all scientists, but far more integrally participatory) was recognized, however, the study of the patient by the analyst in the psychoanalytic situation inevitably had to be seen as a subject for study in itself; that is, the two-person situation could be taken as an object of scientific scrutiny" (pp. 587–588). This chapter offers an attempt at such scrutiny. In

Originally published in *Psychoanalytic Quarterly* (1993) 62: 185–205 and adapted for this book.

it, I suggest that certain relational features, inevitably following from the conditions of the psychoanalytic situation, make a significant contribution to the mutative process of a psychoanalysis. My focus is on particular relational features that are tied to the act of interpretation itself.

In previous writings (Pine, 1981, 1985, 1990), I have looked at development in terms of specific moments—often though not always of high affective intensity—that have significant organizing or formative effects. Here, I look at the moment of interpretation similarly, through its cognitive, affective, and relational features and in terms of its effect in the psychoanalytic process. My point is that certain relational factors have their primary effect at the moment of interpretation (the interpretation activating the relevance of the relational feature) while, in turn, the interpretation has its maximal effect because of the presence of the particular relational feature. The two go hand in hand.

Psychoanalysis: The Process in the Situation
Arlow and Brenner (1990) see analyzing as the essence of the psychoanalytic process, and I concur. Analyzing involves breaking things (here, mental products) into their component parts. The analyst ordinarily accomplishes this through words, in the form of interpretations. The effect of such interpretations is to "destabilize the equilibrium of forces in conflict within the patient's mind. This leads to growing awareness and understanding on the part of analysands of the nature of their conflicts, i.e., their forbidden wishes, self-punitive tendencies, irrational fears, and defenses used to contain them" (Arlow and Brenner, 1990, p. 680). Such destabilization leads, optimally, to the emergence of new material and new understandings, and gradually to psychic change. "The range of the ego's control is expanded. The patient begins to change. This is the essence of the psychoanalytic process as we view it" (p. 680).

As an aside I note that Arlow and Brenner see the component parts that the analyst addresses as drive derivatives ("forbidden wishes"), superego derivatives ("self-punitive tendencies"), and ego derivatives ("irrational fears"—that is, anxiety and the defenses that are used to contain it). But the same view of analytic process as destabilization, emergence of new material, and progressive ego control could hold unaltered were one to see the components differently—for example, as internalized object relations, or even as painful self states. Although Kohut (1984) had a different view of the change process, in principle one need not shift the view of the process even if one were to shift or expand the view of the significant mental contents that analysis addresses.

But the question of how the process brings about change, even in the Arlow and Brenner model, requires further elucidation. These authors note:

> There may be specific, individual elements in the analyst or in the analytic setting that in one case or another serve to evoke and intensify the nature of the transference, such as physical appearance, national or social background, professional positions, etc. In the same spirit, no one would dispute that, in any given analysis, there are nonanalytic factors that militate for or against therapeutic success. To consider these factors part of the psychoanalytic process, however, is quite another matter. They are not an essential part of the course of psychoanalytic treatment, which is what we understand the term psychoanalytic process to mean. (1990, p. 682)

There are many such factors that are unique to specific analyst-patient interactions and hence cannot be viewed as "an essential part" of the psychoanalytic process in general. But other features of this relationship are part of the essence of the psychoanalytic situation and process. These relationship factors are in fact universal, not idiosyncratic, parts of a psychoanalysis, and my aim is to highlight their role in the change process and to contrast them to idiosyncratic, non-specific, and iatrogenic relational characteristics.

The "psychoanalytic situation," as I refer to it, is ordinarily one of frequent patient-analyst contact in a setting where the patient lies on the couch and defines him or herself as seeking the analyst's help with some problem. The patient's free association is matched by the analyst's evenly suspended attention, or as much of each as can be attained. The analyst is reliably present for sessions and consistently focuses on the patient. The analyst's behavior is ordinarily governed by the triad of neutrality, abstinence, and anonymity, with the current recognition that none of these principles can be anywhere near absolute.

No definition of the psychoanalytic *situation* can create a sharp line between it and the psychoanalytic *process*. The situation is not static, and once it is in movement, so to speak, it is already a process. Thus, once the patient is free associating, we have a process, though we may say it is even more of a psychoanalytic process when the patient can shift easily between experiencing and observing, or when the associations flow readily between past, outside present, and transference. Similarly, once the analyst is interpreting, a static situation has become a process. But none of that defines the crucial element of the psychoanalytic process: specifically, what it is about this "situation" and its "movement" that brings about change. This is the piece of the psychoanalytic process that we aspire to understand. It cannot be handled by giving a definition, but only by clinical-theoretical conceptualization. Arlow and Brenner (1990), for example, in the quotation presented earlier, give destabilization of the patient's old conflict resolutions a central place. I highlight an additional feature, already implicit in the literature, concerning relationship-interpretation interactions.

The psychoanalytic situation, which Freud evolved early on, turned out to be a magnificent research instrument. Like the microscope or the telescope, which brough new observations into view, the psychoanalytic situation brought into view the in-depth workings of the human mind, especially through the process of free association and the phenomenon of transference. In light of our current understanding of one-person and two-person psychologies (Modell, 1984), or of alone states and interrelational states, we can appreciate in new ways the innovation of the couch as part of this research instrument. For the couch provides the patient with the optimal opportunity, considering the two-person situation of the analysis, to turn inward, alone with his or her inner experiences, or to turn outward, addressing and relating to the other person in the room. Thus, to the degree that any one situation can provide both, the situation of the patient on the couch provides the opportunity for alone issues and relational issues alike to enter the analytic space. In addition to the place of psychoanalysis as a research instrument, the psychoanalytic situation is also a powerful therapeutic instrument.

The sheer intimacy and intensity of this relationship from the patient's side—deriving from the frequency, reliability, and isolation of the contacts, and from the patient's self-exposure through free association in an inherently unequal relationship—guarantee in most instances that the analysis will matter immensely to the patient. This is the setting both for transference developments and for the patient's receptivity to interpretation (the latter, of course, encountering resistance as well). While Gill (1984) argues that it is the interpretation of the transference that distinguishes psychoanalysis from psychotherapy—more significant even than the use of the couch or the frequency of sessions—it is not inconsistent with his point of view to say that transference developments are likely to be more intense and clearer, hence more subject to interpretation, in the setting of frequent sessions and use of the couch.

Brenner (1976) points out that transference is ubiquitous in all relationships, and Arlow (1984) states that the

> analytic situation does not create the transference. Transference is not a set of special regressive phenomena induced by being a patient, by lying down, by having someone give undivided attention, or by baring one's secrets in an unbalanced, unequal situation [all features of the psychoanalytic situation]. Any of these factors or all of them may be significant, provided they have some resonance with the patient's basic unconscious fantasy, provided they reflect some specific, not general, aspect of the patient's personal history. What can be revived in the transference is only that which is persistently active as a dynamic force in the patient's mind. (p. 26)

Nonetheless, it is not inconsistent with either Brenner's or Arlow's position to state that the built-in features of the psychoanalytic situation are likely to enhance the focus of transference attitudes on the person of the analyst, to bring them into clearer focus, and, of course (because other relationships do not ordinarily allow this), to permit their investigation through interpretation. The psychoanalytic situation, with the features I described, is the setting in which intense, often transference-related things can happen, the events we know as the psychoanalytic process.

These are the general underpinnings. Let me turn to the specifics, the moment when an interpretation is offered. I work with a narrow definition of interpretation: the analyst, through words, calls the patient's attention to some interconnection in the patient's mental content or functioning that the patient, until that moment, had not been fully aware of. Working with the idea quoted earlier (Arlow and Brenner, 1990, p. 680), I focus especially on the workings of interpretations when they "destabilize the equilibrium of forces in conflict within the patient's mind." Interpretation, in this sense, is an element of the psychoanalytic situation-as-setting and of its process of change.

Strachey's (1934) paper on technique provides a model. (I do not use his idea that only the transference interpretation is mutative, but I draw on his discussion of why it is mutative.) Seeing pathology to a significant degree in terms of internalized persecutory objects, reflections of archaic superego functioning, Strachey views interpretation in this domain as producing a dual effect. The first is the clarification (by interpretation in the transference) of the patient's fantasies, expectations, or wishes for persecution at the hands of the analyst on whom the parallel internal objects are projected; the second is the simultaneous experience of the real (interpretation-giving) analyst as benign and nonpersecutory. It is this contrast that makes for the powerful change-inducing effect of the interpretation. Since such a contrast can occur only with a transference interpretation, Strachey puts such interpretations at the center of the change process.

Several features of this situation merit discussion. First, one does not have to subscribe fully to Strachey's view of psychopathology to recognize the significance of his point. We are all aware of how frequently patients experience interpretations as criticisms, as moral condemnations. This is a central feature of pathology, even if not *the* center. Nor do we need to assume that all patients experience the analyst as a benign superego, one that can be progressively internalized so that inner condemnation lessens over time. In fact, I implied the opposite when I just noted how frequently patients view interpretation as criticism. But I would suggest that the process develops in the direction of the analyst's being seen as noncondemning. This occurs in fits and starts, with much backpedaling, but it is the work of interpretation itself that moves it in the direction Strachey suggests.

As Strachey conceptualized in his 1934 paper, the analyst does not have to do anything special beyond ordinary interpretation to achieve the position of benign superego. This does not imply any self-conscious role-playing or interactive efforts. Yet the analyst-patient *relationship* is crucial here. It is the co-occurrence of the cognitive clarification and an *experience* in the analyst-patient relationship—the actualized contrast of the patient's fantasy and the analyst's noncondemning stance—that produces the maximal therapeutic effect. This aspect of the relationship derives from the psychoanalytic situation itself and specifically its feature of analyst *neutrality*, not from any role-playing by the analyst. Noncondemnation is central to neutrality.

At the moment of which Strachey writes, the interpretive factor and the relationship factor are inseparably linked. Each requires the other. The interpretation can have maximal effect because the noncondemning relationship belies the patient's inner world. Additionally, the relationship factor has maximal effect at the moment of interpretation. It is not, I suggest, the analyst's general benignity that produces the change in the patient's inner world in this view, but his or her benignity at the moment when it counts—when the patient's forbidden wishes and expectations of attack by conscience are at center stage.

This model of (1) a simultaneously occurring interpretive factor and relationship factor, the two inseparably linked, (2) the relationship deriving from features of the psychoanalytic situation itself (here, neutrality) without the analyst's having to do anything special to bring it about, and (3) the interpretation requiring the relationship factor for maximal effect, while the relationship factor works most powerfully at the moment of interpretation, is the one I draw on for my next two points as well.

Winnicott's (1963b, 1971) discussion of "survival" readily leads to a second instance parallel to the model described. In the infant-mother relationship, the mother repeatedly survives the infant's destructiveness, thus enabling the infant to learn that destructiveness will not destroy, can be safely and gradually owned, and can be expressed even toward loved ones. The prototypic situation is one where the infant's rage leads to destruction of the internal object (see McDevitt, 1975); but the external mother's soon-reappearing smiling face assures the infant that destruction has not happened. Contrast this to infant rage followed by maternal depression, withdrawal, or matched rage, wherein the infant would presumably learn that its rage has terrible consequences and is unsafe.

The analyst, too, continually "survives" not only the patient's rage but also his or her sexual seductions. The patient in analysis, through both repeated experiences of rage and one or another form of seduction directed toward the analyst, and through observation of the analyst's matter-of-fact response, learns that "nothing happens"—no action, no seduction, no condemnation, no retaliation. Just survival, going on with life, going on with the analysis. While at times this leads to disappointment, further provocation, fantasied condemnation, or wished-for sexual or aggressive action, as analysis of these responses continues, what remains is survival. Life goes on, now with formerly taboo wishes more fully owned.

Here I make similar points to those described earlier: (1) this is not all of analytic change, but is an important moment in it; (2) not all patients experience the analyst's nonretaliative or nonseduced response as being just that, and not all settle for that without trying harder, but the process moves in this direction as interpretation continues to clarify wishes and the analyst's reciprocal anger or sexual actions do not follow; (3) the interpretive and relational factors in these analytic moments are interactively and productively linked; interpretation can have its effect maximally because the analyst does not respond in kind, and the analyst's quiet survival has its maximal effect when interpretation makes clear the patient's wishes for the analyst's reciprocal participation; and (4) the analyst need do nothing special to bring about his or her own "survival" with its implicit message to the patient—no role-playing, no special change of style; "survival" in this sense derives directly from features of the psychoanalytic situation itself, in this case, the analyst's reserved listening and interpretive stance in general and his or her *abstinence* in particular.

A third example following identical lines can be drawn from Loewald (1960). He describes an analysis, including perhaps especially the analyst's interpretive interventions, as producing a series of mini-disintegrations in the patient. This seems to be another way of describing what Arlow and Brenner (1990) refer to as destabilization of the equilibrium of forces in conflict in the patient's mind; their formulation emphasizes the structural disruption, and Loewald's emphasizes the patient's anxiety: two sides of one coin. The point of Loewald's work that I am drawing into my argument, however, is his suggestion that it is because of the patient's safe relationship to the analyst that the mini-disintegration can not only be tolerated but lead to productive work—new content, new insight, new functioning— all gradually, of course. Loewald sees the safety of the patient in the relationship to the analyst as modeled on the mother-infant relationship or, one could say, after Winnicott (1965), on the "holding" environment. I have no problem with this view, but some think it too great a stretch of the developmental analogy (see Modell [1984] and Abrams [1990] for relevant discussions). For the point I wish to make, however, no developmental assumption is necessary; it is sufficient to think of the analyst's provision of a context of safety in contemporaneous terms, rather than in developmentally reactivated terms. That context would still allow tolerance of and work on the mini-disintegration.

Once again this instance of therapeutic impact follows the model I have been describing. Not all patients, of course, and no patient at all times, experience the analytic setting as safe and the analyst as a supportive presence. But these need not be all-or-none matters. To a considerable degree, the analysis moves in this direction over time, sometimes slowly, as conflicting parts of the patient's experience are understood. But specific therapeutic impacts accomplished at moments of disintegration-plus-safety need not be canceled by subsequent experiences of the process and the setting as unsafe. Over time, small gains, achieved piecemeal, are consolidated. Here, too, I am not addressing a general atmosphere of safety but a specific relational feature of the provision (or the patient's sense) of safety at the moment of destabilization. Again, the two are inseparably intertwined; interpretation is able to be effective because of the context of safety, and the context of safety matters especially at the moment of anxiety. And finally, once again, the analyst need do nothing special to achieve this context of safety. The safety flows from normal analytic concern or derives from the analyst's reliable presence, continued attention to the patient (which itself is built on the analyst's own relative anonymity), abstinence, and neutrality—all defining features of the psychoanalytic situation.

These are certainly not all of the change processes in the psychoanalytic process, but I believe they are highly important in it. They bear on superego modification (Strachey), wish and urge (Winnicott), and ego integration (Loewald), the full panoply of the structural model. In the sense that the relational (or interactive) features described both *derive from the psychoanalytic situation* and have a crucial effect *at the moment of interpretation* relevant to one or another of them, I would suggest, in contrast to the Arlow and Brenner argument quoted earlier, that they are an essential (inherent, inseparable, and indispensable) part of the psychoanalytic process, precisely when the process is built around interpretation and destabilization of old modes of conflict resolution.

To summarize this main point, then, certain relational features of the psychoanalytic situation are essential to the workings of the psychoanalytic change process. These begin with the intensity, inequality, and self-exposure of the situation for the patient that enhance the presence and clarity of transference manifestations and guarantee that the analyst and what he or she says will matter to the patient. Beyond that, while the general features of the analyst's interpretive style and overall personality affect the process in endlessly individual ways, specific relational features of the psychoanalytic situation have an essential and general role to play in relation to interpretation. By contradicting the patient's wish, fantasy, or expectation at the moment of interpretation of drive or superego derivatives, they add a direct experiential impact to the already affectively laden cognitive impact of interpretation. And by producing a reliable context of safety, they permit the patient, at the moment of destabilization (Arlow and Brenner) or mini-disintegration (Loewald), to reintegrate in progressive ways. None of this happens automatically. Patients vary in how they experience the analyst. But when things go reasonably well, interpretation moves the process in the described directions, at least at times. Again, none of this requires special role-playing by the analyst; it all follows from the conditions of reliable presence, focus on the patient, neutrality, abstinence, and relative anonymity. And finally, I have highlighted the effect of the relational context at the moment of interpretation. While abstinence (nonparticipation in the patient's sexual and aggressive enactments) and noncondemnation may in general be beneficial for analytic work, and while (depending on one's point of view) general benignity and anonymity may or may not be beneficial, it is not this general impact that I am discussing. Rather, my focus has been on the relational context of the interpretive act at the moment of the patient's encounter with the interpretive content. With regard to this, I can say epigrammatically: interpretation is necessary but not sufficient for change; the analytic relationship is necessary but not sufficient for change; but together, at specified moments, they are both necessary *and* sufficient to bring about change.

Some Comparisons and Contrasts

Abend (1990) states: "Optimum analytic technique demands that the analyst attempt, insofar as possible, to limit his or her activities to observing and analyzing patients' mental functioning. No other mode of intentionally influencing the patient except through the medium of neutral interpretation is to be thought of as analytic, although patients are surely always influenced by other aspects of their experiences with and relationships to their analysts" (p. 539). A few points are worth noting in relation to this statement. First, Abend's proscription of other modes of "intentionally influencing the patient" reflects a widespread, and often justifiable, concern with suggestion, manipulation, use of charisma, artificially planful corrective experiences, and other noninterpretive modes. The relational features I have described are "intentional" only insofar as they are part of the psychoanalytic situation as we aspire to create it. Second, "neutral interpretation" is itself a relationship feature and is part of what I have attempted to bring under scrutiny here. And third, we all share Abend's recognition that patients are always influenced "by other aspects of their experiences with and relationships to their analysts." There are always idiosyncratic features of the patient, the analyst, and the patient-analyst pair that make for unique effects. These are, I suggest, inevitable in any analysis, perhaps even crucial in any particular analysis, but, because of their idiosyncratic nature, not essential to the analytic process in any general or universal way. My concern, by contrast, has been with relational features that are general and essential to the psychoanalytic process.

Boesky (1990) adds to the discussion by taking a strongly interactive view of the psychoanalytic process, but explicitly aiming to approach this via a "one-person psychology." His method is to examine what goes on in the patient when the patient (inevitably) fails at free association, and in the analyst when the analyst (equally inevitably) fails to maintain evenly suspended attention with a focus on the patient. The analytic process that evolves for a particular patient is always affected by this mix in some way, to the degree that "the manifest form of a resistance is even sometimes unconsciously negotiated by both patient and analyst. I am suggesting here a kind of adaptive or benign iatrogenic resistance" (1990, p. 572). Boesky takes pains "to distinguish such a focus . . . from Gill's (1979, 1984) views about the origins of the transference in relation to the patient's plausible perceptions of the analyst's behavior" (p. 576). Boesky also makes clear that he is "not imputing mutative factors to the relationship with the analyst, as compared to interpretation. . . . Further, these issues are in a very different frame of reference than the polemic argument that the analyst must do many things in addition to interpreting, such as providing encouragement, sympathy, or hope" (p. 576).

Though what Boesky is reaching for does seem to be different from the process Gill has stressed, his focus as well as Gill's seems to be in the category that I refer to as idiosyncratic effects—that is, effects that vary for every patient, analyst, and patient-analyst pair. As I noted, such interactions are inevitable in a two-person process, but since they are so variable they are hardly "essential" to the process in general. In contrast to Boesky, I believe that there are factors in the relationship of analyst to patient that are mutative and *universal* in the psychoanalytic process, embedded as they are in the relationship defined by the psychoanalytic situation. They are indeed familiar, have been written about before, and are those that I have summarized. But they do not involve any special provisions of "encouragement, sympathy, or hope"—which neither an object relations psychology nor a two-person interactive view of the process require—but rather are intimately tied to interpretation itself.

Boesky's description of the development of a "benign iatrogenic resistance" brings to the fore another area of relational impact in the psychoanalytic situation; this issue is, I want to make clear, well beyond the topic Boesky was discussing in his paper. It is an area of impact that is neither essential (as I have put forward) nor idiosyncratic, as referred to in various ways by the authors thus far referred to— Arlow, Brenner, Abend, Boesky, and Gill. I have in mind here quite general or potentially general features of the analytic relationship that have an iatrogenic effect but that nonetheless cannot be considered an essential part of the psychoanalytic change process. For example, the use of the couch with the analyst behind it has its potential iatrogenic effects dictated by the particular relationship it creates between patient and analyst. Thus, Broucek (1991) has suggested that the lesser attention to shame than to guilt in the analytic literature (until recently) is in part a function of the absence of the face-to-face encounter (the prototypic situation for shame—averted eyes, blushing) in the analytic setup. In contrast, the "voice of conscience" over your shoulder is closer to the psychology of the analytic situation. In any event, these are yet other relational features of potentially significant impact. They are, however, more artifacts of the psychoanalytic situation than its intended impacts; they are not beneficial in themselves unless and until they enter into the interpretive work.

A last point, stimulated by Boesky's (1990) paper, has to do with the arguments for a noninteractional view advanced by some participants in the discussions of psychoanalytic process to which he alludes. One of the points made in these discussions, according to Boesky, is that we can never say what impact the analyst's behavior is having on the patient because this depends on the patient's individual experience of it. Hence relational features are at best secondary. The patient's dynamics are always primary because they determine the way the analyst will be experienced. I certainly recognize the individuality of patient responses: the way we are experienced, the experience of our voice tone, and the way the content of interpretations is heard vary markedly from patient to patient. This is a fact of life in daily analytic work. Nonetheless, I have argued that, in the regions discussed earlier, the process gradually moves in a direction such that the analyst's noncondemnation, or survival (that is, continued abstinence), or reliable presence is sufficiently experienced at a sufficient number of significant moments for the change processes I have described to take effect.

This follows from our belief in change itself and in reality testing. The patient can learn.

Dewald's (1990) contribution to the *Psychoanalytic Quarterly* symposium is closest to my own view. He writes: "At the level of regression that the patient is experiencing, the analyst's response represents a reaction different from what the patient had anticipated. . . . This leads to increased awareness in the patient of the inappropriate nature of the transference expectations and requires a different form of response" (p. 701). Dewald adds that "by maintaining the analytic situation and optimal abstinence in regard to transference provocation, the analyst demonstrates repeatedly the safety of the structure of the analytic situation and thereby encourages the patient's experimentation with new modes of expression or adaptation" (p. 702). With specification of diverse areas of such impact, with emphasis on the *momentary* significance of relationship-interpretation interactions during the interpretive process, and with elaboration of the characteristics of the psychoanalytic situation that underlies them, my main point is essentially an expansion of this aspect of Dewald's paper.

Concluding Remarks

When two chess grandmasters sit down to play, they focus on the game, but a lot is happening between the two personalities as well. The same goes for two world-class tennis players. Whether it involves grandmasters, world-class athletes, or merely analysts, an intense two-person "game" involves the participants in significant interactions around the activities and rules of the game. The concept of transference was Freud's first entry into explication of this area; analysts have been writing about it in countless ways since his time.

This chapter is a contribution to that discussion, taking the two-person situation as "an object of scientific scrutiny" (Compton, 1990, p. 588). Such scrutiny was a long time coming in psychoanalysis, largely because of the fear that suggestion would be seen to be the motor that drives psychoanalytic change. But in recent decades efforts to scrutinize the analytic relationship have become a virtual flood. Heimann's (1950) work on countertransference and Gill's (1983) work on the analyst's contribution to the transference are prototypes. A recent paper by deJonghe, Rijnierse, and Janssen, "The Role of Support in Psychoanalysis" (1992), argues for the presence not only of mutative interpretation but of mutative *experience* in the analytic relationship, as I do here. The aim of all such scrutiny of the two-person situation can only be to heighten awareness of the situation, tools, and impact of the analyst, and thus to enable the recognition, modulation, or interpretation of such impacts when the situation requires.

When Freud developed the psychoanalytic situation, he developed a magnificent observing instrument. He also developed a powerful situation for interpersonal impact. If it is wrongly applied, we know that can lead to trouble. Our guidelines for the psychoanalytic situation, our personal analyses, our sharing of knowledge, and our personal ethics are all forms of increasing the likelihood of beneficial outcome of engagement in the process.

In its basic structure, the psychoanalytic situation has the core characteristics for facilitating a progressive change process. To describe this, I expand on some of the developmental considerations I alluded to earlier. The infant and young child thrive in the atmosphere of safety that the mother provides, the so-called holding environment (Winnicott, 1965). It includes such things as meeting the infant's needs, modulating stimulation so that it does not become overwhelming, and altogether reliably responding to the infant. But were we able to envelop the infant in such an environment, to meet its every need, surely we would stunt the development of those active and autonomous features that make a person a full human being. Fortunately, the child's biologically programmed thrust forward (say, into bodily self-control, crawling, walking), as well as the caretaker's inevitable failure to meet every need, insures that the child will not stay wrapped in a holding environment that becomes a prison.

An analytic patient is not a child; an analyst is not a mother; and an analysis is not a home. But the reliable backdrop of safety and the appropriately timed opportunity for and expectation of autonomous functioning, which foster the earliest developments of the person, foster development (or change) lifelong. And an analysis does include its variants of these two features. They are part of the background of the analytic situation; they are the stage on which and through which the action happens and which, in fact, enable it to happen. The contemporary backdrop of safety, echoing perhaps the young child's "holding" environment (but at least as different from it as similar to it), refers to the analyst's regularity and reliability, to his or her attention devoted to the patient, to the whole agenda as the patient, who is at the center of concern. And the analyst's attention to the patient's anxiety level, recognizing that analytic work does not go on optimally in circumstances of affect flooding, is the analytic counterpart to parental modulation of stimuli so that the infant is not overwhelmed. The analytic setting provides the place where one can try out not only inner exploration and change and loving but also hating and seduction and rebellion and autonomous activity itself. But no patient experiences an analysis as simply a safe, "held" place. Quite the reverse. We ask the patient to work hard, to venture into threatening inner places, and to carry a significant responsibility for the process. When Freud gave up hypnosis and moved toward free association he was enhancing patient autonomy and activity. Free association is the patient's daring activity. Loewald (1960), as noted in Chapter 3, also points out how the patient's effort to reach the analyst through words sometimes entails finding words for inner experiences for the first time—creating a revised inner life and giving it shape in the act of verbalizing about it. This mix of the analyst's provision of "safety" and the patient's requirement of "autonomy" is, I propose, the ideal mix for insight and change.

Beyond this general relational setting of an analysis, I have tried to show specific areas where relational features deriving from the psychoanalytic situation itself interact with interpretations at the very moment of interpretation in ways that move the psychoanalytic process forward. We barely notice these relational features, so used are we to operating in the psychoanalytic situation in ways governed by the concepts of neutrality, abstinence, relative anonymity, and general reliability. But these defining features of the psychoanalytic situation are themselves forms of relationship. And, as the process moves forward and a patient gets to sense the analyst's noncondemnation, "survival," or safe presence (at least at times), these features of the analytic relationship enhance the impact of interpretations. The analyst's neutrality insures that the patient's (interpreted) fantasy of condemnation will be (experientially) contradicted. Abstinence insures the same for rageful or seductive wishes. And the context of safety makes possible those reintegrations, following from mini-disintegration or destabilization, that mark analytic progress.

In the last two chapters I have addressed in diverse ways aspects of the mix of interpretation and relationship in producing the therapeutic impact of psychoanalysis. In Chapter 5, I turn to a quite different region of psychoanalytic technique: the workings of the ego in the session. This marks a return to issues that were central in discussions of technique in past decades, but I hope to show that they have lost none of their relevance today and that they retain a freshness that enhances our understanding of the variables that make up the analytic process. Because ego processes are often so starkly visible during the course of development, I introduce each of the three areas of discussion with the case of a child in treatment, and then go on to the relevant issues and illustrations in work with adults.

5 The Ego in the Session

For some analysts ego psychology has a bad name, whether because of psychoanalytic politics (a wish to disavow the so-called classical position) or because it appears to leave the "depths" of the mind behind or because—as a nonexperiential concept—"ego" does not have the appeal of, say, sexual or aggressive urges, affects, repetitive object relationships, or subjective states. "Ego" is an indispensable concept, however, and central to all clinical work. At the very least, the concept helps us in any assessment of a person's capacity to enter and participate in the analytic task. But much more is addressed by the concept "ego." In this chapter I use clinical vignettes to illustrate three of the ways in which the ego makes its appearance in sessions: first, in terms of the achievements and failures in its developmental history; second, in terms of its participation in the work of the analytic process; and third, in its more frequently described role in defense in relation to some intrapsychic disturbance. Each discussion will center on clinical judgments within the session.

I use the concept "ego" to consider the person from the standpoint of defense, adaptation, and reality testing: defense in relation to experienced dangers in the internal world, adaptation to the expectations and perceived realities of the external world, and reality testing in relation to both internal and external and to the capacity to know them in themselves and to tell them apart. The term *ego* is shorthand; it need not be reified; it always refers to *the person's modes of managing psychic life and the world*.

If we did not have an ego psychology, it would be necessary to invent one, and Freud (1923, 1926) did just that, followed by Anna Freud (1936) and Heinz Hartmann (1939). Hartmann expanded the ego concept greatly, and some of these expansions enter into my clinical discussion. But Hartmann's conceptual and aclinical style also contributed to a turn away from ego psychology in the current era of primary focus on technique. Ego concepts need not be aclinical, however, and in Anna Freud's writings they were part of a living clinical process. I try to write here within that tradition.

A psychology of ego function was indispensible for Freud and was present in his writings before it was formally conceptualized as such. It was clearly present in nascent form in his concepts of defense and repression (Freud, 1894), concepts that were necessary for him to use in order to explain what he was seeing clinically. Years later (1926) another clinical observation, that anxiety seemed to *precede* defense rather than follow it as a conversion of blocked libido, led to his signal theory of anxiety and thence to a concept of a stronger ego—an ego that could call the pleasure principle, in this case pain avoidance, into play on the side of defense and against the instinctual drives. Also, as I noted in Chapter 2, the requirements of Freud's theory in itself led to an ego psychology: since the system Unconscious and, later, the Id are timeless and do not learn, some means was needed to explain learning and change, in the analytic process as well as in life. But the ultimate requirement for an ego psychology stems from our position in evolution. We are not outside of evolution, and evolution would not have produced a creature with no adaptive capacities; that would not serve survival of species.

As I have tried to make clear throughout this book, my own recent clinical work has been heavily influenced by current psychoanalytic theories of technique and of mind. But I wish also to demonstrate that an ego psychology, while certainly not the new wave, is as relevant as it ever was and central to a full understanding of issues of technique. I have chosen to use as my main clinical examples instances readily subsumed under the structural theory. I believe, however, that the ego concept is relevant to every extant theory of mind; each involves issues of defense, adaptation, and reality testing though they vary in their conception of what it is that is defended against—that is, the nature of the intrapsychically experienced danger or pain.

Developmental Achievements and Failures

Billy, age seven and the only child in a cleanliness-oriented household, was still soiling fairly regularly when he began treatment with me. The symptom was maddening to his parents. Three years later, by age ten, he had given up the soiling, at least in part through work he and I did together. I describe three incidents (widely spaced over the three years), each of which confronted me with questions: Was this an alternative (displaced) expression of the symptom or was it more socialized or even a sublimation? How much "ego work" had been done by him? And, depending on my answers, should I intervene or not, and if so, how?

One day toward the end of the first year of treatment, Billy came in sadly complaining that his parents had taken away his new gun—a gun, he explained, that shot little paper pellets. They said he was making a mess all over the house with the pellets. He said he was having fun; the gun was supposed to shoot pellets. Of course I noted the messing in this story (to myself). And I also knew that, though he was at times ashamed and depressed about his soiling, at other times he took a provocative delight in "messing," specifically by turning his back on me, bending over, and sending a loud fart in my direction. The gun play could have been another instance of this delight in provocation, but it also could have been a step up—boyish, displaced, better paper pellets than soiling his pants. How should I intervene with him or with his parents? I was uncertain.

Billy resolved my uncertainty in the next session. His parents had given back the gun; he brought it to the session to show it to me. In no time my office was littered with paper pellets. But, more instructively, each shot of the gun was accompanied, as the pellet fell to the floor, by a loud "plop" sound from Billy's lips—and the same impish smile and glint in his eye I had seen after the farts directed toward me. So perhaps some "ego work" in the form of displacement had been accomplished by him, but not much, and certainly not enough; I now had no doubt that he was crapping on my floor and that he knew it. At this point my interpretive stance was clear to me, and I easily showed him (and he readily recognized) that this was another form of soiling. This event did, however, provide entry into discussing his pleasure in tormenting his parents, and he came to see how he was torn between that pleasure and his inner shame and depression.

About a year later, when he had pretty much given up the soiling—though there was still frequent staining of his undershorts and he still inwardly defined himself as a soiler and carried the associated shame and depression—Billy came in with something new to report. He had had an afterschool date with a friend twice that week. He confided to me a "great game" they had developed. They would gather up a large clump of toilet paper, soak it and bunch it up into a wet wad, and try to drop it out the window on a passerby. It was great fun, he let me know. Again I was torn. The parallels to soiling seemed clear enough, but again some displacement to boyish activity had taken place, some ego work, and I thought it likely that he was not aware at the moment of the link to soiling. I saw no real danger to passersby; death by toilet paper wads is uncommon. Additionally the play had a socialized component; Billy, ordinarily a social isolate, was doing this with a friend. I chose to inquire a bit, to listen, and to say nothing.

Again things changed by the next session. Billy came in anxiously, painfully telling me that he had not been able to fall asleep at night. He would lie awake worrying that he had *not* played his toilet paper "game" that day, and he felt a compulsion to get up and "play" it. Clearly this was no longer play. So it now seemed to me that, even if this were a boyishly socialized displacement into play, a developmental step up of sorts, it was not working. After I listened a bit more, and in light of his particular report of anxiety and compulsion if he had *not* thrown toilet paper, I chose to say the following: "Billy, I think throwing toilet paper is like making b.m.'s, and you felt you had found a regular-boy way to have fun attacking people with messes instead of a b.m.-in-your-pants way. That's why you worried if you had *not* thrown the paper. It was supposed to prove you were a regular boy. I think you're still worrying about yourself even though you don't make in your pants like you used to." He looked at me with recognition and relief; following this exchange the symptom that was in the process of being created (the compulsion that kept him awake) disappeared, and our work went on.

Then again, about one year later, another incident in this series occurred. Billy told me he had started a penny collection; he had hundreds of them. I thought I recognized the old symptom again in the little copper pellets, but this time they were *collected* and seemingly a big step beyond the "plop" of paper pellets or the tossed toilet paper wads. Here, I thought, real transformative work had been done intrapsychically; a sublimation had evolved.

Another incident took place a few sessions later. I opened the door to my waiting room for his session and there he was. Also in the waiting room was an adolescent boy waiting to see my office partner. Billy had a beaten-up brown paper bag on his lap and was hunched over it, holding it together; I soon learned that all of his pennies were in it. He looked distraught. As soon as he entered, still hunched over and struggling to hold the bag together, he explained in a pained voice: "Dr. Pine, I brought my pennies to show you, but the bag started to tear and the pennies almost spilled. It would have made a big mess. That big boy would have thought I was such a baby!" So here we were again. But this time I made a different choice based on my assessment of Billy's ego functioning within the total situation. I judged that this time he had absolutely no awareness of any link to his soiling; I considered that the penny collection was an age-appropriate sublimation; and I felt that *any* link I made between the penny collecting and the soiling, however well intentioned to help him with the momentary eruption of shame in the waiting room, would or at least could lead to an invasion of the sublimated activity by the soiling ideation, thus spoiling it. I therefore said only: "I'm sure the big boy wouldn't have thought badly of you. Anyway, I'm glad you brought your penny collection. Let me see it." And later I gave him something more secure to carry the pennies home in. I assumed that, were there subsequent breakthroughs of soiling-related ideas, urges, or affects into the penny-collecting, I would have later chances to deal with it either similarly or differently, depending on my assessment of his ego functioning at the moment. But it did not come up again.

With some patients, at some times, depending on how the clinical material seems to fall at the moment—but not as a general rule of technique or as something always in the forefront of my consciousness—I am working with a concept of the ego and its development that helps me to conceptualize what is going on and whether and how to intervene. I have just illustrated that closely with Billy, where in three incidents I found myself questioning whether the soiling and associated affects or some more socialized, displaced, or even sublimated activity was at the center, reflecting transformative ego work. Related matters, suggested by a concept of the achievements or failures of ego function and ego development at various ages, come up in numerous ways. I illustrate a few, but more briefly.

Issues parallel to those with Billy arise with adults in analysis with respect to sublimated activities. Writers, painters, but also graduate students writing dissertations, or persons involved in the more mundane activities of daily work or living—each scenario, when going smoothly, may teach us something about the person but is more likely to attract attention and require interpretive work when interrupted, when anxiety or shame or doubt invades the activity or when the activity becomes otherwise blocked. For some individuals, interpretive work with smoothly functioning activities is experienced as intrusive or reductive; it can sometimes actively corrupt certain otherwise ego-syntonic activities when their establishment is tenuous or the person involved is fragile. This is not always the case, and we learn in the doing which patients can work interpretively with well-functioning, ego-syntonic activities as a source from which to learn, without its interfering with the activity.

This view has much in common with the interpretation of play in child treatment. Since the child is ordinarily not knowingly *intending* to communicate through the play, interpretations can be intrusive and lead to termination of the playing. One can almost always safely interpret a child's play when it has been disrupted by some negative affect or by the associations it has stimulated; in this situation, the interpreter can come in on the side of the ego to make play possible once again, or to relieve the anxiety. So too with the timing of intervention with respect to sublimations and their disruption, as with Billy and his paper "plops," his toilet paper game, and finally—but in reverse (noninterpretation)—his penny collection. The assessment of level and intactness of ego function guides the timing and form of interpretation.

The examples I have given from Billy's treatment can be thought of in terms of the construction of a sublimation. Related issues can be described from another standpoint as the achievement of secondary autonomy in relation to activities born out of early conflict but now having a life of their own in the present. To view them only genetically can lead to losing touch with the patient. Let me give a nonclinical example from a recent *New Yorker* article (Seabrook, 1996).

Steve Redgrave is a gold-medalist Olympic rower, part of the English team. For specific physiological reasons, rowing at Olympic-competition speed levels is an excruciatingly painful activity. When asked about it, however, Redgrave denies the pain. The question has come up whether Redgrave, now thirty-five years of age and old by Olympic standards, will retire after the 1996 Olympics. His wife, who is also the physician of the English rowing team, doubts it. What drives him on?

> "Oh, I don't know," she said. "I suppose it comes from his dyslexia, his learning disability. That made it very difficult for him in school—until he found rowing, which was something he could do well. The others he went to school with who had that problem had to face it earlier, but because of Steve's rowing he never had to, and now it's a bigger problem, because he put it off that long. Rowing's given him an avenue away from facing it."
>
> Steve disagreed with this. "If I don't stop rowing, it's because I love to row. My dyslexia is not a factor." (Seabrook, 1996, p. 35)

His wife interprets in terms of the past. Redgrave himself says, in effect, that rowing has aims, values, and pleasures in the present. Analytically, we are often aware of both and have to guide our intervention (or nonintervention) according to the success of or intrusions on ego function as experienced by the patient at the moment.

Issues around the loss of autonomy in what should be the primary autonomous ego apparatuses of perception, memory, thought, motility, or affect also come directly into sessions. I illustrate this with material from two adult analyses where there were intrusions on the autonomy of an *entire mental function*, not just anxiety or blocking around specific mental contents.

Arthur was an isolated, obsessional, and affectively dry graduate student in engineering who was, in spite of these traits, devoted to his analysis and made good use of it. Here and there, when a question came up about spontaneous fantasies or daydreams, he showed himself to be averse to them. Even more striking was that the same aversion applied to spontaneous memories. Of course he had memory; he remembered how to get to my office each day, for example, and how to speak the English language. But a concrete memory *spontaneously* appearing in his mind was greeted aversively, and he generally denied having any. He rationalized this pathetically: "I'm young. I live in a neighborhood filled with young people. We look towards the future; we're not interested in the past." I shall not go into this in any detail except to describe the turning point that culminated in its resolution— that is, a gradual return of the ability to permit spontaneous memories and fantasies. We were speaking one day of this aversion to memories when a memory burst forth from him. He recalled having worked as a dishwasher at a nearby luncheonette while in college. One day, late in the lunch hour, the dishes from the noontime rush were being carried in by the trayload by the waiters. "They were coming so fast I was afraid I'd be buried by the slop." That was it. Not a memory of some early trauma, but an indicator of, or a metaphor for, what the fear of memory was about: that memories would come so fast (and be so awful) that he would be "buried by the slop." By drawing on this now explicitly verbalized fear and fantasy, I was able over time to enable him to have spontaneous memories and daydreams and to work with them analytically.

In another patient, it was independent thought that was interfered with. Though his work as a high school teacher obviously required planning and communicating and thinking, in the analysis he disclaimed any of his own quite significant contributions to the process, reattributing his thoughts to me. It turned out that, among other things, *thinking* on his own had come to signify *being* alone. Fears and sadness regarding object loss (his mother had died when he was a young child) underlay much of the blocking in the use of an entire ego function: independent thought.

One last clinical illustration of the utility in the session of a concept of the ego and its developmental failure derives from when I was supervising a therapist-in-training who was working with Aaron, a ten-year-old boy. I thought at second hand that Aaron seemed phobic and essentially in the neurotic range. But his anxiety did not come under control through what seemed like good therapeutic work, and his fears spread now to this and now to that in a panphobic way. To get the feel of the child, I arranged to meet him through the premise of being a consultant who would work with the boy and his mother jointly for a few sessions. I was not with Aaron twenty minutes before I became convinced that his anxiety was of the overwhelmed panic-anxiety sort, not a bound phobia with some affective spillover. There had not been, as I could then formulate it, the development of a successfully working anxiety signal that could trigger in-place defenses. Rather, anxiety "signaled" only that more anxiety was on the way, and it escalated to a flood almost instantaneously. In the session, when his anxiety grew and disruptive, frantic activity developed along with it, his mother started scolding him. I intervened and told her (in his presence) that he could not control himself at the moment, that he was overwhelmed and needed her help, and that her scolding was not useful. (As an aside, our exchange was interesting. The mother immediately became indignant. "You mean I shouldn't express my feelings?" she said. I responded: "Exactly. At least not right now. He needs your help." She instantly replied: "I'm in therapy myself and so are a lot of my friends and we're all learning to express our feelings, to let them out." "Yes, but not right now," I said. "Aaron is overwhelmed and needs to feel you are in control and can help him get under control." Her final reply: "I never heard of such a thing!") In a subsequent session, when the anxiety again began to flood and his mother again began to scold, Aaron (in a voice desperate, pleading, and in pain) said to her over and over: "You heard what Dr. Pine said. You heard what Dr. Pine said. You heard what Dr. Pine said." Unfortunately, although *he* did, she did not.

My point in this first part of this chapter has been that, as illustrated by the case of Billy and the eventual emergence of a sublimated activity, the analyst or therapist is aided by having a concept of the ego and its development, that is, of the evolution and workings of the anxiety signal and defense and sublimation, of the maintenance of the primary autonomy of the ego apparatuses, and of the achievement of secondary autonomy in some activities—or failures in any of these. Modes of understanding are enhanced by such concepts, and interventions and their timing are in turn shaped by the understandings.

The Patient's Participation in the Analytic Exchange

The clinical examples I have been describing, involving recognition of achievements and failures in the developmental history of the ego as evidenced within the session, are specific and not always a focus of the work. By contrast, in this section I want to discuss a problem of general significance in sessions: the person's readiness, in ego psychological terms, to hear, work with, and contribute to the interpretive process. I again start with an example from the treatment of a child: eight-year-old Sophie.

Sophie had come to me some two and a half years before the events I recount. The only child of recently divorced parents, she was both lonely and, as her parents described it, "overexcitable." The parents were on good terms with respect to the handling of their child, and both expressed concern about the impact on her of the divorce and of the events that preceded it—events I need not go into. She also was said to create sadomasochistic games with her pet cat and her Raggedy Ann doll; her parents were worried about this—rightly so, I thought. From my first contact with Sophie it seemed clear to me that her "overexcitability" was an expression of her tendency to leap into excited action with overelevated mood the moment she had the slightest hint of any uncomfortable feeling; it was a form of defense through action.

In the first two years of the treatment, my main work was to enable her to *experience* feelings, to know them mentally, which again is ego development work, as I discussed in the prior section. We had made considerable progress in this area, though it was variable. About three months prior to the events I describe next she had come in reporting a nightmare. I explained to her how we could work as detectives, using the dream and her thoughts about it as clues to figure out what the dream was about. By this point she was able to participate in this work, even saying, "But what about this part of it?" halfway through the work on the dream, and greeting my final interpretation with, "Now I think you got it!" (Recall that she was only eight years old.) The dream led to her reporting a childhood secret (whether it had been available as a memory before and withheld, I do not know) and the related unraveling of a longstanding severe situational anxiety response, which has shown no sign of its presence since that work.

Now for the material I wish to report. Remember, this child formerly, and still at times, fled into excited action at the slightest distress. Reference to the sadomasochistic games and anything even close to sex or bodies was met with immediate flight. My aim is to discuss a patient's signaling readiness—conceptualized as an ego activity—to participate in the work in some particular area.

Sophie came in one day armed with a new joke. "Why did the man swim in the ocean?" "Why?" I asked. "To make peepee in it." End of joke, but the start of a long series of events in the sessions. She spent the rest of the session making drawings. One of them had what seemed to me a clear representation of male genitals; a second led to spontaneous verbalization on the same theme. I had simply made note of each one aloud as we went along; she listened but did not flee. At the end I recounted the common theme in the joke, the drawing, and the verbalization. She clearly saw it, expressed a mix of curiosity and distress in the tone of her "I don't know why," and hid her face in *contained* and focal embarrassment and without flight into activity.

In the next two sessions there was much related material, which I need not review. My point is only that she stayed with it, though she did say toward the end of one session: "You're a crazy man." I asked why. "To talk with a little girl about things like this." I heard real trust and affection in her statement, though puzzlement and concern also. I said with a smile: "It must seem strange, but it's something that's on your mind for some reason."

Sophie spent alternate weekends with one or the other parent, and the following weekend was her father's turn. He called me at about 7:30 on Monday morning to say that Sophie had had a bad dream and wanted to tell it to me. I was impressed that she wanted to bring it to me, and we spoke right then on the phone. Here is the dream as reported: "I was in bed with my daddy and a bad guy came in and shot me. The bullet went through my arm and stuck in my clothing between my elbow and my shoulder. I had to do a somersault to get it off. And then I woke up." I told her I was glad that she called to tell it to me, and that we could work on it in her session (later that day), just as we did with the other dream.

We did work on it. I need not describe her associations or my questions and interpretations. My aim is to detail her *ability* to participate in the work. The talk went to nakedness, to intercourse ("My parents don't do it!"), and to my interpretation of an overall sexual meaning. I did not bring anything into the transference. Her response to the interpretation, with playful mockery and yet recognition, was: "You solved it (the dream that is), but I don't like it!" Nonetheless she came back the next day (the last in this sequence) and said: "We didn't get it all yet. Why did he shoot me?" This led us into the sexual meaning of the shooting and a punishment meaning. She greeted this with: "Now we got it! [pause] Oh! I wish I had never told you that joke!" (about peeing in the ocean). With this remarkable statement she was showing that she had a grasp of the continuity of the whole sequence of the work though spread over several sessions, was feeling the discomfort, and was containing it.

To top this, after a pause she said spontaneously: "You're torturing me with talk about sex. I'm going to cut off your peepee and my daddy's." I told her I could hear in her voice that sex talk was like torture and said it reminded me of the games she played with her cat and her Raggedy Ann doll. I wondered if she thought sex was like torture (there was a specific basis for my asking this, which I shall not give here). Her response: "No! [pause] Is it? [pause] For who? Both people or just one?"

Altogether a remarkable sequence in an eight-year-old who formerly had fled all discomfort, was unable to mentalize things, and instead rushed into action. She showed a well-functioning ego and a capacity to participate in the work at each step along the way: in her recognition of the sexuality in her drawings ("I don't know why"), in her playful and trusting comment (in spite of discomfort) that I was a crazy man "to talk about such things with a little girl," in her calling me to tell me the dream, in her recognition of when we "got" the understanding of the dream, and in her capacity then to ask, "Is it torture? For whom?" And, of course, her capacity was also shown by her staying with these themes for some five sessions spread over two weeks.

Many things lead to the decision to interpret: the expressive content itself, some optimal level of anxiety, the presence of some transference manifestation in the material. But I am here focusing on just one aspect: the indicators of a patient's capacity to self-observe and to hear and take in the analyst's words—ego functions. The same kind of assessment may result in quite different intervention decisions, and next I illustrate some of those briefly.

Several years ago I was working with a forty-year-old man, a mediator by profession and not by chance. He played, or sought to play, the mediator role in his physically violent family during his growing-up years. For the first couple of years of treatment, his own anger was notable by its absence. But then, in a half-dozen widely spaced sessions in our third year of work, I felt sure I was hearing explicit references to his anger, past or present. Each time I addressed it with a question or comment, however, he vigorously criticized me for pushing my own agenda and reading it into what he was saying, and then he withdrew. Only later did an understanding of the situation develop between us. He had, he later came to realize, semi-consciously made a pact with himself as a child: he would survive by mediating and never entering the fray himself. What I thought I heard as indirect communications about anger with an inner sense of (ego) control he experienced as alien and dangerous slip-ups, at least at the point at which I took note of them. Only after we spent considerable time on the childhood pact he had made with himself—that is, the defense aspect (to be the mediator only)—could his self-observation and analytic participation come into play in relation to the anger itself.

A second kind of situation involves observation of intact ego function signaling to the treating person a nonreceptivity rather than a readiness to explore. Some years ago, before pharmaceuticals rapidly cooled off psychotic processes in patients entering psychiatric hospitals, one would not infrequently see a therapist who had become fascinated by the exploration of bizarre psychotic thought processes and would feel the loss of it and find the work less interesting when the patient reinstituted what were often tight controls and became quite dry. Not infrequently a therapist would try to reach back into the psychotic thinking with the unsurprising result that the patient withdrew, got angry, got frightened, or, in the worst instances, slipped back into the disordered thought. Here, a surface of intact ego function signified not the readiness to explore, but an effort to blot out all mental dangers. Time enough to explore when the patient, without prodding by the therapist, began to slip; at such times, some patients, frightened by the possible return of the psychotic thinking, could welcome exploratory interventions that had the intent of clarifying things in order to reestablish control.

A third kind of example occurs sometimes when we are working in the midst of an intensely rageful, sexual, envious, or other transference struggle that is paralyzing the work. We work in the transference because it has the most immediacy and therefore the most heat, but if it is too hot work can be impossible. No work gets done when the observing ego is swamped and loses its autonomy in the face of whatever passion is active. Often it is useful in such a situation to move the work elsewhere, to the past or the outside present (around the same issue), to cool off the situation enough to make self-observation possible. This is a variant of something I wrote about earlier under the heading "strike while the iron is cold" (Pine, 1984). There I referred to fragile patients or to moments in any treatment when interpretations could not be received (during conditions of great affective intensity) because the experienced danger to intact ego function was too great; interpretation in the form of education-like clarification could sometimes be made in a subsequent session—looking back—after the storm had quieted. In the instance of moving interpretation out of the transference, we could say we strike *where* the iron is cool*er*. In all my examples I am trying to show how an assessment of ongoing ego function, particularly in the form of the observer capacity, guides intervention or helps us refind our bearings when we go astray.

A final, more general point, at the level of theory of technique, further entails addressing the patient where his or her observer function can be operative. In his central body of work, Paul Gray (1994) stresses the importance of staying close to the analytic surface and thus working where the patient can become aware of what is going on. He does this by proposing that we listen for the drive derivatives in the patient's associations and then taking note to ourselves and to the patient of his or her flight from, undoing of, reaction against, or other resistance to that content. I am here addressing that same technical point. My disagreement with Gray is that he narrows the field of the work too much in assuming that the relations between drive derivatives and defenses are the principal contents of mind for analysis. Fred Busch (1995), working similarly to Gray, broadens the field by suggesting that we keep an eye on the analytic surface for *any* sign of distress, without presuming that it is in response to drive derivatives. This leaves room, in my terms, for distress also in relation to repetitive object relations growing out of strain trauma from the childhood era, or painful subjective states of self around deficits in parental care, or feelings of humiliation or helplessness in relation to defects in ego function. But the overall thrust of the discussion is the focus on the area of mental function with respect to which the patient can come to see and know what is going on inside.

A discussion related to both Gray's and Busch's points took place between Theodore Jacobs and André Green at the Congress of the International Psychoanalytic Association in 1993. Jacobs had presented process notes of a session. Green, the discussant, was critical of Jacobs for not going deep enough, not interpreting various things that had been implied in the patient's associations. Jacobs's response was to the point. He said, in effect, that "going deep" means going where the patient can still recognize what you are saying and where it draws from (self-observation); Dr. Green's "deep" interpretations, Jacobs suggested, would be mere words, in essence promoting intellectualization and not "deep" at all.

Intrapsychic Defense

Eleven-year-old Johnny, whose presenting problems at a city hospital clinic included clowning behavior sufficiently compulsive that it had contributed to school failure, was seen by a supervisee of mine in twice-weekly psychotherapy. The clowning behavior and other symptoms had erupted after a series of separations. The first separation was brought about by the child's removal from his home by a city agency following maternal neglect and paternal abuse. He went to one foster home and then to the homes of a series of relatives, none of whom kept him for long, in large part because of his other symptoms—encopresis and collecting things from street garbage cans that he would store under his bed. He was now living with his maternal grandmother, who was also threatening to move away with another grandchild, leaving him behind. The incident that follows addresses the clowning behavior and the separation issue.

Johnny had rapidly grown attached to his female therapist and, in numerous ways, demonstrated his wish to make the office his permanent home. Now, several months into the treatment, in the session I draw from, his therapist had asked him to tell her about his memories of his several shifts of home and what these homes and the shifts had been like for him. Johnny spoke articulately and with surprising readiness; he had not been very expressive before. He focused especially on his time with his mother and father. The details are not necessary for the point I wish to make, except to note that he reached the point of saying, quite movingly: "I'd give anything to be back with my mother!" This was immediately followed, his therapist told me, by a plunge into a joking, clowning attitude. The high point of the clowning was his rapidly pulling any available junk from his pockets while saying: "I'd give *anything*—even these paper clips, even this spool, even these candies!" The therapist told me that she immediately saw the clowning here as his driven effort to escape the pain of longing consequent upon his recalling his life with his mother and expressing his wish to be back with her. It is of interest (though a side point) that this beginning therapist also told me that she chose to say nothing to the boy, in large part because (as she recognized) she was herself uncomfortable with the degree of his pain and longing.

Thus far we see a simple and straightforward example of defense against inner distress. While the defense concept initially came into use to describe defense against drive derivatives (such as fantasies or wishes), Anna Freud (1936) explicitly extended the concept to include defense against affect; and later, Arnold Modell (1984) extended it to include defense against object relations. Perhaps the strongest and most unifying formulation in this domain was offered by Jacob Jacobson (1994). He suggested that the common conceptual ground that binds diverse psychoanalytic theories of mind together is the centrality of theories of painful affect. From this perspective, psychoanalysis centers on a view of the mind as beset by painful affect that has to be coped with (defended against, managed) in some way. Psychoanalytic theories differ in terms of what they see as the nature and source of the painful affect and the means of dealing with it, but the task—defense against affect, as seen in eleven-year-old Johnny—is essentially the same in all psychoanalytic models.

Johnny's session continued. About ten minutes later, he started talking about videotapes. He said that he and his mother used to watch videotapes together. To the therapist's "Tell me more," he added: "We would watch and joke around; we had a lot of fun when we did that; we would get silly together." The student therapist did not pick up the link until I pointed it out, but what have we here? Suddenly the joking as a defense against painful longing appears in a different light. Now it is readily seen as a repetition of a (perhaps only imagined, perhaps real) pleasurable part of the lost object relationship with mother, a means of actualizing in the present the memory of "joking around" with his mother. So, if we go back, the sequence is as follows. He says, "I'd give anything to be back with my mother" and then, via his joking ("even these paper clips, even this spool"), he transports himself (probably without full awareness, perhaps marginal awareness—we do not know) back into the situation of the imagined and longed-for relation to his mother. He has simultaneously protected himself from his pain and, in this clowning way that is quite automatic for him, fulfilled his wish; clowning has placed him back with his mother.

Is one of these two views of his "joking around"—the defense view or the object connection view—more "true" than the other? In this instance, I think not. I believe he could have responded well to interventions from both points of view, experiencing their intrapsychic "rightness." If they were worded properly, I believe they could have become usable for him without simply worsening his pain. I shall suggest some interventions in a moment, but first some further discussion of the intrapsychic defense aspect of the ego in the session.

Ordinarily, we think of defense in the session not as something having "thing" quality, not a defense "mechanism," but as a moment in a process, a way the clinical material can be organized at that moment. It is not the case that the possibilities for such organization are unlimited; "anything goes" does not go well. But there is usually more than one way to understand the associative material of the session that can be useful in moving the treatment forward. Interpretation in terms of defense, as modulating unpleasant affect or fleeing or disguising thought content, is often one of those ways.

We no longer think of defense as simply a sign of "resistance" that must be gotten through in order to get to the "real" content. Defense is understood now as a reflection of the person's mode of coping, of functioning in relation to the internal world. As such, it is at least equal in significance to any other part of mental life that is to be explored in a therapy or analysis. While Breuer fled analysis after his experiences with transference (his patient's falling in love with him), it was one of Freud's great achievements to turn the view of transference upside down and find it to be not a problem requiring flight, but one of the invaluable routes into the exploration of the patient's psyche. Concepts of resistance and defense followed a parallel path of development in the theory of technique. At first they were seen as something to be gotten out of the way in order to reach the unconscious fantasies and wishes reflective of infantile sexual drives. Later, with the development of an ego psychology, defense and resistance came to be seen as direct expressions of core features of the person that were themselves to be understood. And, with Wilhelm Reich's (1949) work on character analysis, they came to be seen as central features of characterology. Today, when most analysis is character analysis, defense and its expression in the so-called resistance are at the center of what analysis helps the analysand to see in all its functions, its rigidities, its maladroit self-defeating efforts at adaptation (when these are indeed the case), and its history.

When Johnny said, "I'd give anything to be back with my mother" and immediately shifted into his joking mode, and considering that he was an abandoned and neglected child and that the loss was real, I would have intervened in a way to enable him to hold onto his wish to at least some degree by simultaneously helping him bear his pain. The wish was, after all, a tie to the only mother he had. Bearing in mind that he was quite trusting of and attached to his therapist at this point in the treatment, I proposed that she could have said something like: "I know you started joking because of how hard it was for you when you said you'd give anything to be back with your mother; of course you would like to be back with her; I understand that." Remember that at this point in the session we do not yet know that "joking around" was a way of *being with* his mother. Let me make clear the aim of the intervention as stated. Clowning behavior was getting him into difficulty, including school failure; it was problematic. Though intrapsychically an effort at defense, symptomatically it was maladaptive. Here my intervention has the intention of indicating my understanding of the *function* of clowning (clowning started because the expression of the wish to be with mother was painful) and offering another mode of managing the affect (a defense equivalent) through the current object relation to the therapist ("of course you would like to be back with her; I understand that").

Later, when Johnny's associations went to the video experiences with his mother ("We would watch and joke around; we had a lot of fun when we did that; we would get silly together"), and the "defense" turned out also to be a significant means of actualizing the past relation to his mother in the present, I would probably have made that clear to him as well, seeing this as an opportunity to give him back a piece of his relation to his mother, showing him that he does carry her with him. Thus, I might have said (right after his "we would get silly together"): "Oh! Now I understand something else, Johnny!" (this by way of alerting his attention). "When you started joking before, after you said you'd give anything to be back with your mother, the joking was one of the good ways you *really could* be with her. I guess there are some good memories, and you can hold them with you by joking around." I imagine it would only be a matter of time after this that the treatment could also turn to the compulsive quality of the joking—the clowning behavior—and at least one of its functions revealed here, in order to begin the process of enabling him to give it up in its maladaptive form.

Like the question of the patient's readiness to participate in the analytic work, the issue of intrapsychic defense is relevant at all times and in all sessions. Defense (the modulation of inner distress) is an ongoing part of mental life. Whether it becomes the central focus of the work depends on many factors, including the degree to which it is seen as *obstructing* the analytic work, the degree to which it is seen as *revealing* something important about the patient, and altogether its relation to whatever seems the central issue of the session. Defense is always present; whether it becomes the interpretive focus depends on its place in the hierarchy of affective significance at the moment.

The wealth of intrapsychic issues potentially reached through paying attention to (rather than getting past) defense and its expression as "resistance" in the session is well illustrated in the following treatment of a woman in analysis. She was thirty-five years of age, married and childless, when she came for treatment. She sought help because she both wanted to have a child and feared it. The fear was paralyzing, and it took the form of anxiety-driven obsessive thought: "It will be too much" or "I'll get overwhelmed" or "I'll be out of control" or "It will be too confusing." She had been stuck with this thought for years and could not bring herself to try to conceive. Now, having reached age thirty-five and very much wishing to have a baby, she came into treatment.

Two things became clear as the work progressed. The first was her thinking style in the sessions. Her thoughts would come in a flood. Her ideas seemed dynamically rich, her delivery insightful, but one idea would follow the other, tumbling out in confusing array. There was never a quality of looseness or thought disorganization, but rather of rushing away from each idea, and presumably its attendant dangers, soon after she had given voice to it. In this sense her thinking was quite well organized; she had a reliable and predictably utilized defensive mode available in the face of intrapsychic distress: mental flight. She would come back to many ideas in her later sessions, but they were not built upon and were therefore for the most part useless to her. (There were of course exceptions, but those are not my focus here.) Though the ideas would reappear in subsequent sessions they still seemed not to be "held"; rather, they seemed to "occur" to her, almost to "happen," again and again, before once more being left behind. Excess and flight served as her defense; it was the functional "resistance" in the session that made progress slow.

The second thing that became clear as the work progressed was the nature of her life history as she experienced it. Here too the quality was one of flooding, of "too much." Was this colored by her mode of telling about it? Was there something about her that led to her experiencing it that way in the first place? While neither of these two possibilities can be entirely ruled out, the internal feature of the analytic process strongly supported the view that she was indeed subjected to too much knowledge, too much overhearing of things, too much seeing. As the only child in a household that included her parents, two Don Juan–like maternal uncles, various governesses and other servants, and highly flamboyant maternal grandparents, each of whom had had active and publicly known sexual affairs throughout her growing-up years, she was overloaded with sexual knowledge long before she could assimilate it even minimally. Add to this her own fantasy elaborations and wishes, and the picture of hyperstimulation was complete. So the history, the style in the sessions, and the presenting problem all revolved around the quality of "too much": too much confusion, overstimulation, and experience beyond what she could control. One can see immediately that the "resistance" *is* the life story. Whether it is treated as defense-resistance or as expressive content to be kept in center stage would depend on the analytic moment and how the analyst thinks it would be best approached at that particular time.

To date (the analysis is still in process), the style of flight from ideas (not flight *of* ideas) has been understood in a number of ways: (1) as a protection against being overstimulated by seeing too much, knowing too much, the flight now from her own thoughts about the overstimulating memories, but also directed against thought in general; (2) as a turning of the passive to active with respect to overstimulation, now drowning the analyst as she had felt drowned as a child; (3) as an expression in (verbal) action (on the analyst) of her experience of the overstimulation as an assault; (4) as a mode of being stupid, of maintaining stupidity, of not knowing—something that affected her day-to-day functioning in widespread and limiting ways—and of having this "stupidity" set in especially when she was angry (suggesting her own anger at the overstimulating intrusions, the other side of the experience of being assaulted); and (5) as a participation in the familial mode of denial of what is in fact being revealed and communicated, this denial serving as self-protection and, more idiosyncratically for her, as a way to preserve her idealized view of her father as well as to identify with him and protect him against her own jealousy and rage.

Analysis of "resistance" in a case like this is not intended merely to get past it to something else but to *analyze it*, to understand its component parts and their history and its place in the patient's life.

Let me give one last example of a focus on defense, in this instance a misplaced focus, stemming from the analyst's misunderstanding of what were the patient's primary concerns at that particular point. The analyst's intent was, in effect, to say, "You are talking about this because it is safe and keeps you away from something else." Only in time did the analyst come to believe that the patient was talking about what mattered in a way that mattered, and that she (the analyst) had been endeavoring to impose a particular view of mind on the patient's material (see Chapter 7 for further examples of this kind of error).

I enter this analysis in midstream without giving its history or the patient's history. I do this because my aim is to illustrate a point; I recognize that without full backup material, the reader cannot truly make an independent judgment about it.

The patient, a forty-year-old man who had graduated from law school but never managed to pass the bar examination and was now working in a family business, would regularly come to sessions and talk about films he had seen and things about himself that they had reminded him of. Often these were memories of anger and associated guilt; equally often they were memories of sexual experiences with attendant shame. This material seemed significant to the analyst, though it had no apparent relation to the problems that had brought the patient to analysis (which I shall not go into here). In numerous sessions, the patient would turn from these film-stimulated memories and confessional reports to speaking of his unhappiness with his work in the family business, where (he said) he never got sufficient praise and recognition. He would go into elaborate detail about moments in his life when such recognition had been forthcoming, especially from his many girlfriends, and how precious that had been to him. He would bemoan the lack of recognition that he felt when his analyst was silent, but spoke of how he would feel a glow when his analyst would (as he experienced it) find something of value in what he had been saying (indicated by her making some interpretation).

The analyst had been thinking of these shifts in the session (from anger-guilt and sex-shame to the search for recognition and praise) as a form of backing off, of seeking to feel valued in spite of the "confessions," of shifting to safer areas—in short, as a resistance that the analyst would interpret to enable the patient to "get beyond" it and arrive at some other place (the anger-guilt and sex-shame issues). Only gradually did the analyst turn her understanding around a full 180 degrees. The analysis took a decisive step foward when she came to the belief that the self-esteem issues (reflected in the search for recognition and praise) were the primary ones and that the reports about sex and anger reflected the patient's attempt to please the analyst and get "recognition" and "praise" from her.

The concept of intrapsychic defense evolved within a particular theory, Freud's theory. I have already suggested that it must have a place in every psychoanalytic theory of mind; each of those theories includes a central focus on psychic pain, however that is understood within the theory, and therefore the human mind will be understood in part through its efforts to cope with that pain (Jacobson, 1994). But when the mind is viewed single-mindedly, around one set of issues that are seen to be necessarily the main ones (whether this be sexuality or interpersonal experience in the here-and-now or internalized object relations), failures to understand become a real danger. In the reported instance, my guess is that the anger-guilt and sex-shame issues will eventually find their place onto center stage in this analysis, although they are not there at this point. The analyst, working within a particular theoretical model, was seeking to put them there, thereby ignoring the central thrust of the patient's material; hence her view of the self-esteem material as resistive rather than expressive. "Defense interpretation" is central in analytic work, but it is only one part of the full story of an analysis.

Concluding Remarks

What I have been attempting to show is that, seventy-five years after its formal origins (Freud, 1923, 1926) and sixty years after its flowering (Freud, 1937; A. Freud, 1936; Hartmann, 1939), an ego psychological point of view can be—I would say should be—a living presence in the analytic hour. It provides tools for comprehending aspects of what is going on and how and when to approach it. It spawns concepts like ego defect (Pine, 1985, 1990), alerting us to unreliable or distorted or delayed development of defense, the anxiety signal, affect modulation, impulse control, a sense of separateness (which is a part of reality testing), object constancy—all significant achievements subsumed under the concept "ego." It alerts us to one of the ways in which pathology is organized—in incursions on the ego's autonomy—whether these incursions come via object need (as in the patient who feared the consequences of independent thought) or via the "slop" of sexual and aggressive memories (as in the patient with the aversive response to spontaneous memories and daydreams) or in numerous other ways.

Though not illustrated here, ego psychology offers us the concept of the ego's *relative* autonomy—not either-or—such that the autonomous function of memory, thought, or the like may be seen as present at one moment and absent at another, a concept with major implications for the timing and focus of interpretation. It can alert us to another aspect of the relativity of autonomy (also not illustrated here)—the "how much" dimension: not too hot, not too cold, but just right. We have all seen instances where the "autonomy" of thought, for example, is so complete (so separated from affective and wishful sources) that the thought process is dead and dried out, with all affective energy eliminated from it (a caricature of autonomy), or where it is so animated, so suffused with wish and urge, that it suffers distortion. An ego concept also gives us tools for distinguishing between well-functioning defenses, sublimations, or other adaptations and their breakdown, again with implications for the when and how of intervention. It supplies a multitude of ways to recognize when the patient has enough observing ego to receive what is offered interpretively. And, in its most familiar role, it offers a conception of intrapsychic defense and of resistance within the analytic process, now seen to be equally significant for what they reveal and what they obscure.

Work in these ways, around and with a concept of the ego and its functions, is not what I believe analysis *is*. It is not the interpretation of defense before impulse. It is not the finding of creative ways to work with ego defect (Pine, 1990; Fleming, 1975). It is not interpretation in the transference. It is not reconstruction. It is not the processing of countertransference reactions or the interpretation of transference-countertransference enactments. It is not a focus on the here-and-now relationship of two people in interaction. And it is not a focus on the patient's current psychic reality or subjectivity. It is *all* of these things at *some* times, and any one or more of them at particular times and with particular patients.

An ego psychology is a necessary part of all theories of contemporary psychoanalysis, even though it had its conceptual birth in relation to a particular theory. Whether we view the mind as powered by sexual and aggressive urges and fantasies, internalized object relations, painful subjective states, or something else, problems of defense in relation to intrapsychic life, of adaptation to the outside world, and of reality testing all remain. An ego psychology addresses them. And we have conscious minds, capable of planning and anticipating and judging. So we have to recognize that we are powered not only by what is in the depths but also by rational thought, and that too is recognized in our concept "ego."

Ego psychology retains a firm place in the psychoanalytic pantheon in relation to both the multiplicity of current theories and the central current focus on technique. Having illustrated that here and having also previously discussed relational components of the therapeutic impact (in Chapters 3 and 4), I now turn to a subject that draws on both aspects: questions regarding (ego) defect and (object relational) deficit in development and treatment.

6 Conflict, Defect, and Deficit

Among the phenomena that become important during any psychoanalytic treatment, conflict is every*where*, but it is not every*thing*. In this chapter, I discuss two "things" that may become prominent in any particular analysis—defects and deficits—things that themselves get involved in conflict.

I advocate no either-or opposition with regard to conflict, on the one hand, and defects and deficits, on the other. But defects and deficits exist in the real world (and therefore in our patients) and have an impact on the course and the outcome of analyses; hence it is in our interest to conceptualize them clearly.

I am well aware that any view of what is in the "real world," let alone a particular patient's historical real world, is speculative at best,

Originally published in *Psychoanalytic Study of the Child* (1994) 49: 222–240 and adapted for this book.

and probably in principle unknowable. Here I am trying out some ideas as they have developed for me in my clinical work, and pointing out along the way some of the uncertainties and ambiguities to which they give rise. The working definitions and clinical judgments I give have turned out to be useful in my clinical work. I offer them here as a contribution to an ongoing discussion in the literature.

Definitions

Conflict refers to the opposition of two or more intrapsychic aims. In terms of Freud's structural theory, this is most commonly understood with regard to the opposition to drive aims imposed by the ego's anxiety signal and defenses or the superego's condemnation—that is, intersystemic conflict. But conflict can also be intrasystemic: drive aims that are simultaneously passive and violent, or destructive and erotic; ego aims toward achievement and success coupled with defenses operating against that very success; conscience that condemns, but simultaneously permits, particular acts. With the advent of object relations and self theories, we can consider an expanded range of intrapsychic conflict: thus, an individual may simultaneously cling to and flee from a painful self state (such as low self-esteem or self-hate) or may simultaneously fight against and hold on to (for its familiarity and security) some old internalized object relationship. A particular sought-after object relationship may regularly produce a degraded sense of self—the one sought, the other being both attractive and aversive. Or a sought-after object relationship may produce a chronically overstimulating sense of sexual arousal. The combinations producing intrapsychic conflict are endless.

A *deficit* involves an insufficiency of appropriate input from the surround—ordinarily from the primary caretakers. Thus, it is like a bank deficit; not enough has been put into the (intrapsychic) bank. Since there is always *some* input (even if silence, absence, or hate), this view of deficit is actually based on the presumption that optimal human development requires an "average expectable" (Hartmann, 1939) or "good enough" (Winnicott, 1960) input, without which progressive development is slowed or distorted and the subjective state is painful.

The particular "deficits" I discuss most centrally here have been placed in the foreground of psychoanalysts' attention largely through Kohut's (1971, 1977) writings. They could not have been absent before, and no doubt many a clinician worked with them in some tactful way to further a particular analysis. But in articulating them more clearly and relating them to transference manifestations, Kohut made it possible both to use these phenomena clinically and to discuss them theoretically. Kohut at first emphasized deficiencies in two areas in particular: insufficient "mirroring" of the child (with its consequences for primary self feelings, self-worth, and the experience of oneself as a center of initiative, an active agent) and insufficient provision of opportunity for the child to idealize the parent(s) (with its consequences for both the formation and the taming of goals, values, and ideals). These are surely not the only significant and potential deficiencies of parental input. All the progressive steps in the development of control, displacement, and sublimation of impulses, the reliability, flexibility, and maturation of defenses, and the clarity, strength, and, ultimately, benevolence of conscience require some participation of the primary caretakers, whether that is the general nonspecific assistance of their facilitating environment (Winnicott, 1965) or more specific acts and inputs that provide the basis for identification and other forms of learning. This is always part of the total psychic field in which the child's intrapsychic constructions are being built. Perhaps we can understand Kohut's contribution to be a clarification of the necessary inputs (and the related deficiencies or deficits) for the optimal development of the "narcissistic sector" of the personality. But other inputs are critical to the formation of impulse control, affect tolerance, the differentiation of affects, the development of a stable array of defenses, and movement toward trust, toward signal anxiety, and toward object constancy, to name a few.

Deficits of parental input exist. What is their result? How do they come to be represented in intrapsychic life? I suggest that they may be formative of *defects* (defined later); they may become internalized and reenacted as part of the array of repetitiously relived internalized object relationships; and they may also continue to be felt as ongoing painful subjective states of self, which I shall refer to as "raw wounds."

Whereas deficiencies or deficits refer to phenomena (insufficiencies) in the relation of the person to his or her caretaking surround, *defect* refers to something that is not working well (such as something that is broken). It is within the person, not the person-caretaker relationship, no matter how it got there. In fact, I restrict my use of the term *defect* to the domain of ego function—that is, to faulty development of aspects of defense, adaptation, and reality testing.

The justification for thinking that defects, like deficits, "exist in the world" is simple and straightforward. Adults all have capacities for defense, adaptation, and reality testing that infants do not yet have. Hence, these capacities must have developed along the way. Anything that develops can develop poorly or well; I refer to those faulty developments that are in the region of defense, adaptation, and reality testing as (ego) defects. The sources of defects are wide-ranging. A defect may stem from a deficit—that is, deficient input in some area. For example, reliable parental care ordinarily produces trust that gratification will arrive and hence the capacity for delay; a *deficit* in such reliable care might then produce a *defect* in the capacity to delay. Or a defect can stem from some biological condition (blindness, neuropsychological learning difficulties) that handicaps some aspect of development. Further, early conflict resolutions that have the effect of stunting ego development can produce "defects" in one or another area (see Mahler, 1942, on pseudoimbecility, or Youngerman, 1979, on elective mutism). Whatever the source, the residue is some significant failure of development in an aspect of ego function: adaptation, reality testing, or defense, or some combination of these.

Deficit

Any faulty (depriving, destructive, overstimulating, contradictory) parental provision can be conceptualized as producing a deficit for the child in his or her optimal experience of some more benign and developmentally forwarding version of those provisions; this is merely an object relational experience formulated in "deficit" terms. Further, object deprivation (through death, divorce, or separation) or sensory deprivation (through blindness, deafness) can also be readily seen as creating certain kinds of deficits in the child's experience; these are familiar phenomena.

By contrast, I focus on a clinical phenomenon wherein the patient feels intensely that something good was not given or that something bad was wrongly given by the parent(s). And though we cannot (and ordinarily, I believe, need not) establish the objective reality of what was or was not given, it is that intense feeling of a need-not-met or something-wrongly-given that turns out to be a crucial center of the pathology—in these cases, of psychic pain (the "raw wound"). Thus I am working with "deficits" defined by how they appear during the course of an analysis, rather than by how they may or may not have occurred in the individual's personal development.

I believe these are among the phenomena Kohut wrote of. In recent years, I feel I have been seeing them clearly for the first time. I have no doubt that the phenomena were there all along, but I am able to listen differently and to conceptualize more variously today than when I began analytic work. I wish to discuss them here in my own terms and ways. My debt to Kohut's work will be clear, though I weave into and out of his ways of thinking without specifically highlighting the points of likeness or difference.

For reasons of confidentiality, I do not give much clinical detail but simply list some of the phenomena to which I refer. This will be sufficient for my main purpose, which is to call attention to a set of phenomena that I can then discuss in terms of various clinical and theoretical issues.

I am thinking of patients for whom being heard or being taken seriously (or the experience of not being heard or taken seriously) is an affectively powerful, central experience. Or of patients for whom having their sense of reality confirmed (usually with regard to assessments of family interactions and pathology)—in contrast to the denial or hypocrisy that experience tells them had characterized their past lives—is similarly powerful and central. Or of patients for whom having their sense of boundaries respected and not being intruded on or invaded is central (I am not here referring to resistance to getting into painful areas but rather to situations in which the crossing of boundaries *is* the painful area that characterized the patient's history). Or of patients for whom being left too much alone with their inner pain (an experience sometimes precipitated by analytic silence) produces a devastating sense of deficiency in the environmental provision. Or of patients for whom not being displaced from center stage is the central issue—this "displacing" experienced in the analytic process when the analyst either offers transference interpretations or (sometimes) offers any interpretation at all (either of which can be experienced as a demand to share the stage). Or of patients for whom not being controlled or put down or shown up is a central issue—any of these experiences stemming from the act of interpretation itself, and mirroring too closely, as the patient perceives it, experiences with the parents-of-childhood.

Analytic tact ordinarily is sufficient to ensure that the patient can feel adequately, and not intrusively, attended to. But for the patients I am discussing here, these experiences come to seem overwhelmingly central. Violations (through the analytic process itself) of the wish or need (to be heard, confirmed, kept in the center of attention, have one's boundary integrity respected) produce rage or disintegration experiences; the reaction to the experienced violation is intense. By contrast, respect for the need (when that somehow becomes noticed and not simply background) produces gratitude or integration—also an intense reaction, though a quieter one. Though I list the core phenomena simply (being heard, and so on), in no instance did the patients I am referring to have clear words for these feelings when we began the analysis. They emerged and became formulatable through experiences in the analyst-patient interchange, experiences either of violation or of recognition (producing rage and disintegration or gratitude and integration).

In my experience these phenomena are not universals. While I see no reason to doubt that something of the sort exists in everyone to some degree, for many it is background, and the ordinary good-enough analytic relationship meets, and does not violate, the patient's specific wish or need. But for some, these experiences become central to the work and become the pathway to the understanding of significant parts of the patient's history (as experienced), now relived in the transference relationship. Consistent with this, such experiences are notably patient-specific, one or another of the phenomena being the crucial one for any particular patient. It is for such patients in particular, as I understand my experience with them, that empathic failure (Kohut, 1984) becomes a central issue in analysis: failure is signaled by the rage or disintegration response to an experience of the analyst's violation of the particular wish or need. "Empathic failure," in this sense, is not a "mistake" of the analyst (though I do not mean to excuse clumsiness) but is rather a phenomenon inevitably present for those patients who have high vulnerability in the listening and taking-in relationship and process as they go on between patient and analyst. Although one should not aim to produce such failures (and need not, for they will surely occur spontaneously), it is nonetheless true that a considerable part of the actual work of the analysis takes place in relation to these very "failures"—coming to be able to recognize and understand their meaning to the patient, to know their history in the life story, and to overcome them (repeatedly) in the analytic interchange (thus creating a new contemporary "history"). The work here is both relational and cognitive. It involves failures, corrections, and refindings within the patient-analyst relationship as well as understandings of the between-persons (present and past) and within-patient workings of the whole experience.

In contrast, for some patients, some aspect of what the analyst may experience as average expectable analytic listening and tact provides a central, reorganizing new object relationship experience that (in my observation) moves the analysis forward in surprising and individualized ways, which enable the patient to articulate, often for the first time, some experienced deficit in the parental provision. In Chapter 3 I referred to two such instances—of a patient's feeling heard for the first time and another's discovering reliability (nonloss) of the other through the analyst's regular appearance at sessions. These are not things we "do" for the patient; they are what the patient finds in what we *are*. We could not prevent them should we wish to, because they reflect longings or need states that the patient unknowingly carries into the transference. Again, there is no forced choice to be faced regarding "relationship-effect" versus "insight-effect" in the work. For, as I have seen this, it regularly happens that it is an aspect of the *experience* of the analytic relationship (as retraumatizing or as better-than-the-past) that permits the patient to *discover* a previously unverbalizable (or at least unverbalized) aspect of his or her experience of personal history, and then to be able to work on it, and its effects, with understanding. The internally integrative effects of the better-than-the-past experiences can be powerful; the same can be said of the painful retraumatizing experiences when they are discovered, named, explored, and worked through.

Though these phenomena are secondarily involved in conflict that also becomes interpretable, they are experienced by the patients as *deficits* in parental handling. "They did not hear me"; "they did not acknowledge my achievements"; "they kept the spotlight on themselves and never gave it to me"; "they didn't respect my privacy"; "they took over whatever I did"—these are variants of various patients' cries. Although I cannot know the actual history, in these instances I came to believe that the patient's rendition of the history was accurate—certainly as to the patient's experience, and probably (I believe) as to significant aspects of the caretakers' behavior.

The patient's specific experience of need (to be heard, confirmed, given the center, not be intruded on) is not equivalent to a need for nonspecific care, concern, or empathy (though the specific need is often "gratified" in the nonspecific good-enough care that analysis provides). The analytic process, even when carried out with optimal sensitivity on the part of the analyst, will create "violations" of the specific needs felt by these patients. It is not as though some wished-for "perfect" technique can avoid them; these *are* the phenomena the patient brings, and in a *good analysis* the patient will find a way to experience them, then to work on them, and eventually to work them through to some degree.

An aside: I have said that the analytic relationship sometimes gratifies the patient's need to be heard, to be in the center, and so on. I do not find, clinically, that such gratification makes for trouble in the analysis, unlike the gratification of a libidinal or aggressive wish. And it is found by the patient, as indicated, in our ordinary good-enough analytic listening and tact. This is more like the meeting of an ego need or a core object-relational need—a basic developmental requirement. When met, it permits the work to go forward more productively, though the "meeting of the need," like the history of the need itself, comes to be verbalized and understood along the way. The technical guideline of "abstinence" was developed in relation to a drive-based psychology of the mind and need not apply equally in certain aspects of the spheres of object relations or ego function. This is not to say that such experiences cannot become involved in libidinal, aggressive, or other conflict. They often do, and work goes on with respect to this. But I maintain that the phenomena, reflecting experienced history, have a central significance in themselves.

And finally, though the emergence of such phenomena is central and significant, I do not find that it shifts the whole nature of the work—say, to a more self-psychological model (Goldberg, 1978). Instead, a many-sided analysis continues, with this as one central element in it.

I would also like to raise a few questions about these clinical phenomena at a more theoretical level. The patients I have described retain a sense of acute pain in relation to something they experience as a fault or deficiency in what they received by way of care from their parents. Because the pain is so acutely felt when something in the analysis touches it in the wrong way, I think of it as a "raw wound." Why is history carried this way in some patients? Let us say, as an example, that a parent regularly views a child with disdain. Why is it that one person will internalize the object relationship and reenact it with others, treating them with disdain, and another person will carry the painful sense of disdain as a raw wound, a wound that can be painfully exacerbated at the slightest wrong touch? One possibility is that it takes a degree of formation and differentiation of a self to internalize and then repeat an early relationship. Lacking that, the experience is carried as a subjective sense of wound. This suggestion points to different degrees of psychological activity. Thus, the internalization and enactment of old object relationships ordinarily involve some cognitive restructuring of the experience, some inner processing, and a turn from passivity to activity. Not so the direct continuance of the sense of injury and vulnerability. This is not to say that such experiences do not undergo alteration and secondary elaboration over time. They do get endowed with "meaning"—they are "explained" via fantasy and idiosyncratic connections—but the sense of being a victim of experiences at the hands of the primary caretakers and, later, others retains affective centrality and power.

The classification of such phenomena as deficits gives attention to what has *not* happened in a good way from the standpoint of the individual's subjective experience. But it is possible to link such phenomena to psychic mechanisms with which we are familiar, such as trauma or, more particularly, strain trauma (Kris, 1956). The experienced impact of the parental failure (by not doing or wrongly doing, as the case may be) leaves the child with an inner experience of aloneness, or invadedness, or cast-asideness, or worthlessness that cannot be mastered. My emphasis is on strain trauma (rather than shock trauma; Kris, 1956), because the assumption is that these situations reflect ongoing patterns of caretaker-child interaction. I assume that single instances of such relatedness are not likely to have sufficient shock power to create trauma but that the additive effect (over years of childhood development) of repetitive forms of humiliating, underacknowledging, controlling, or invading relatedness amounts to an intensity of experience that is not mastered—hence, the continuation of the "raw wound" state.

Given this description, I find no problem in seeing such "subjective states of self" (a term I question in a moment) as primary units of mental life, in Kernberg's (1976) sense. An experience of self and object linked by some affect is laid down in memory in some form as a "unit" that ever after operates intrapsychically, organizing the way experiences are understood and disorganizing the person when the repetition of the trauma becomes too great. Given the patient's vulnerability in the analytic process because of his or her exposure and because of the inequality of the relationship, it is not surprising that there are experiences of the repetition of the childhood strain trauma—moments that, optimally, become foci of the analytic work. The intense psychological slaps experienced by a child whose parent ignores him or her (see Pine, 1990, the case of Mr. E.) or intrudes or regularly steals center stage from him or her create direct experiences of psychic pain that have primacy as "units of mental life." That is, these subjective states are neither epiphenomenal nor secondary to something else but are directly recorded experiences that become organizers; and when the strain trauma has been great enough, they become organizers of a considerable segment of mental life. They then become foci for fantasy formation, self-definition, wish, defensive flight, and interpersonal vulnerability; in short, they enter into the sphere of conflict. As Sandler (1981) has suggested, just as the child has primary needs for safety and care beyond the domain of sexuality, so too there are primary needs for recognition, confirmation, and respect for boundaries: when these are provided, they go almost unnoticed, but when violated become highly visible in psychic life.

And, finally, before leaving the subject of deficits, I wish to give brief recognition to questions regarding the description of the subjective aspects of these phenomena as states of "self." Self psychologists, I believe, would place the phenomena I have been describing in the narcissistic sphere of the personality. This term, as I see it used in the recent literature, seems to refer both (or at different times) to issues of self-definition (boundaries, identity, continuity) and to issues of self-worth; concepts regarding the "integrity" or "discontinuity" of the "self," for example, often contain reference to both. From my clinical work, I have no problem in describing such phenomena as subjective states of self. But I recognize that the term *self* has multiple referents. At times it is used to denote a cognitive construction, as in Spitz's (1957) or Mahler's (1972) work on self-other differentiation. At times it has reference to affective tone, as in aspects of Mahler's work (1966) and in Winnicott's (1965) and Kohut's (1977) writings. Certainly, when we consider self as a representation within the ego (Hartmann, 1950), we are aware that it is a representation molded by experiences in the spheres of drive, defense, object relations, mastery, and affect. As such, it is in a sense a "secondary" phenomenon, an outcome of more basic events.

Call it what we will, there is clearly a primary affective impact of parental handling or mishandling (with reference to the child's needs for recognition, confirmation, and respect for boundaries) that, when too far from optimal, leaves some individuals with a subjective sense of vulnerability with which we, as clinicians, come face to face. Though I do not recommend moving immediately from such subjective reports to a "deficit" view of the patient's pathology (or ever fully abandoning a conflict view), nonetheless, when the ordinary analytic process in these areas is experienced as retraumatizing or, in contrast, as unusually integrative—and when confirming historical material emerges—a deficit view of this aspect of the pathology is crucial to the continued forward movement of analytic understanding.

Defect

I have looked at a deficit in the parental provision to the child as the "cause" of any number of effects (especially of the self state that I have described as a "raw wound"). By contrast, a defect can be viewed as an "effect" stemming from any number of causes: in the parental provision, in the inborn biology of the individual, in conflict resolution that goes awry, or in trauma.

The defects in defense, adaptation, and reality testing that I address are ordinarily subtle and are not obvious on initial consultation. Starting an analysis, as I do, by automatically listening for the repetitive themes, fantasies, wishes, fears, and resistances, often expressed in the transference, I do not ordinarily find myself thinking in terms of ego defects early in the process. But on occasion (certainly not in every instance) and with patients with whom there is an analytic process in motion, a process that continues through to the end, I find myself thinking that some particular aspect of ego function is not fully serviceable for the patient. I have in mind here difficulties in holding onto the idea of the other (object constancy), difficulties in impulse control, difficulties in affect control so that affective flooding occurs readily, or absence of an anxiety signal or of adequate defense so that overwhelming anxiety seems to develop almost instantly in specific areas of the patient's functioning.

I do not come to such considerations rapidly. But with some patients, perhaps after a year or three or more, I may begin to think in such terms. Until that point, I usually work with the relevant clinical phenomena by interpretation and other efforts at clarification and understanding. When I do begin to think in such terms, I usually find that the patient has been trying to tell me about the failure of function in some way all along—not clearly, and not insistently, but nonetheless telling me in some way. When I finally find individualized words for the phenomenon, words that match the patient's experience, I am usually greeted by a response of relief and recognition, a response not unlike the sense of being heard or having one's reality confirmed that I described in the section on deficit. Although the patient's experience may be of (finally) being understood, *what* is understood (a defect in ego function, as I conceptualize it) is very different from the phenomenon of deficit, where what is understood is some experienced failure in the parental provision. In the latter instance, being understood is a first step in ameliorating. In the instance of ego defect, the understanding just identifies the task, which may or may not be achievable.

In the abstract, the concept of "defect" runs us into trouble, for it seems to imply some standard of optimal function that the individual has not reached. In a sense we can have rough standards, because we do know something about what evolution has made possible for the human animal in the spheres of drive control, object relatedness, thought, and adaptation to external reality. But still, the differences in such matters related to personal style, cultural variation, and specific individual potential make it perilous to rely too much on external standards. Such "standards," as in knowledge of what evolution has made possible for human beings, at best alert us only to the possible, not the obligatory, in human function. At that we are probably limited by our own relatively narrow (culture-based and character-based) sense of the "possible."

Clinically, however, we work not in the abstract but in the concrete—in this particular patient's life and thought. Here we find that there are behaviors a particular patient strives for that he or she feels are unattainable, that feel to the patient like a functional lack. It is the patient's sense (as eventually comes clear in the analysis) of some functional incapacity that is our anchor. Of course, there is nothing that should lead us automatically from this "sense of defect" (see Coen, 1986) to a formulation regarding "actual" defect; indeed, we may still be working with something that is essentially fantasy, a compromise formation representing other forces. My contention in this section of the chapter, however, is that there are defects of function that, in particular analyses, are usefully recognized as such, with caution and at some point along the way. (I am not, by the way, referring to a patient's sense that he or she cannot function in some holistic behavioral area, such as work or relationships or sexuality. Rather, I have in mind what we can think of as basic tools of adaptive function, like object constancy, or impulse and affect control, or the development of the anxiety signal, or the move from need-gratifying to specific object relationships, or the developmental maturation of defenses.)

I have discussed the concept of ego defect elsewhere (Pine, 1990) with extensive clinical illustrations, and so I do not go into full detail here. But, for completeness, I summarize briefly two of the cases discussed there.

A thirty-year-old female stockbroker who had made excellent use of the analytic process and of insight still had the sense that she could not control tendencies toward inappropriate sexual action. For four years, much interpretive work had been done in this area, as else-where, but an actual action tendency persisted in spite of the patient's capacity to make use of interpretation in other aspects of the analytic work. By this point in the analysis enough of her history had become known to me to have a picture of various subtle seductions of this patient as a child by parents whose controls were also not fully reli-able. When I reconstructed the history in terms that made sense of the residual failure of control of the action tendencies for the patient (in terms of faulty identifications and experiences of everyday "seduc-tion"), she felt greatly relieved and understood. Two sets of events fol-lowed, both generated by the patient; but I was able to see the use she was making of them and in turn to make further use of them myself.

The first was a period of active (detailed and explicit) sexual fan-tasizing about the analyst that had (as I sensed it) a quality of play, without anxiety or the fear that she would act on the fantasies. By not interpreting the content, as I had in the past, or some aspects of the way it was being used (for resistance, seduction, self-stimulation), which I considered secondary at this moment, but instead underscor-ing the play quality, I was able to foster (or simply allow the patient to achieve) a heightened sense of self-control. Following this behavior, the patient produced a number of mild, almost symbolic sexual actings-out (for example, sending a Christmas card that was a trifle too intimate to the analyst). Again, my recognition that these reflected her sense that she could act and retain control seemed to strengthen the controls she was achieving. During these events (the sexual fan-tasizing and the mild acting out), the fact that I did not enter into the seduction (in contrast to her parents' behavior) gave her a new object relation or a new basis for identification with a figure who could retain self-control. The consequence was that, after about four years of prior analytic work (an indispensable part of the total process), these analytic events and experiences seemed to produce reliable con-trol, which has continued in the five years or so since.

There are no mechanistic solutions to such problems. The patient produced the behaviors, and I was able to recognize their function.

Were I, for example, to try to achieve the same result with another patient by instructing the patient to engage in sexual fantasies about me, I would clearly be engaging in a seduction.

The second case is one described by Fleming (1975), which I discussed from the ego-defect point of view in an earlier publication (Pine, 1990). Here the patient was understood to have a defect in the capacity to hold on to the image of the object. I want to highlight from my point of view some events in the analysis that seemed to modify the defect. The first two of these events were initiated by the analyst, but the patient made use of them in his own way, a way that the analyst could not have anticipated. Much regular analytic work also went on, which, once again, I consider indispensable, but that is not my focus here.

At some point, when the analyst had apparently already begun to think in terms of a defect of object constancy, Fleming, sensitive to the (in part) analytically induced severe anxiety the patient was experiencing at weekend separations, encouraged the patient to associate during the absences in order to understand the anxiety when he was experiencing it. As I read it, the result was that the patient came up not with insight into the anxiety but with the discovery that the process of associating helped him to keep the analyst in mind. (That is, the act of associating, linked to her, enabled him to hold the memory.) This is reminiscent of Piaget's (1937) discovery that prior to the full development of object permanence (for example, remembering and going after a ball that has been hidden under a cloth), the young child could go after the hidden ball if he were already in action, moving toward it, when it was put under the cloth; the action assisted the remembering. For Fleming's patient, the "action" was associating.

The second intervention by Fleming that the patient made distinctive use of also came at a weekend separation, when, again in the face of the patient's severe separation anxiety, the analyst suggested that he could telephone her if needed. He did not call. But on the following Monday he reported that he had instead looked up her address in the telephone book and found the building she lived in. This enabled him to picture where she was and therefore to hold her in mind. She still existed in a real place, and this enabled her to exist for him mentally. (This led to the recovery of a parallel memory in relation to his long-hospitalized mother; he could better keep her in mind after a visit to the hospital, seeing and then picturing where she was.)

The third intervention, actually a nonintervention, came when the patient began a period of getting off the couch at the session's end and staring at the analyst momentarily. Fleming said nothing, sensing that he was working at fixing her image in his mind. (Much later he thanked her for not saying anything at these times.) This is reminiscent to me of the actions (fantasizing, controlled acting out) that my patient initiated and that I saw in terms of her work on impulse control.

In both instances (mine and Fleming's), minor variations in technique were initiated (Fleming's suggestions about telephone calls, my shifting away from the content toward the mastery functions of fantasizing-as-play and action as trial-control). Equally important, we each made use of behaviors the patient brought in (the fantasizing, Fleming's patient pausing to look at her), a use based on a formulation regarding a defect. But each case also represented a full, rounded, and for the most part fairly "typical" analysis. The shifts at moments with respect to the defect view of some piece of the patient's functioning are entirely consistent with the conduct of an ordinary analysis.

Conflict

It is not my aim here to discuss conflict in general, but only the embeddedness of deficit and defect phenomena in a mind in conflict. To uncover a defect or a deficit (or, more cautiously, to formulate a particular clinical phenomenon in those terms) is not to decide that the whole analysis up to that point has been a mistake and that an entirely different way of working is required. Here I get into the interconnections between defects, deficits, and conflicts, between malfunctions and the region of fantasies and wishes, between structures and meanings. This issue has also been discussed by Killingmo (1989).

The mind produces explanations. While in some areas of function these explanations draw on rational problem-solving abilities and the world of reality, in other areas that are more vague, more stressful, the mind's explanations are likely to draw on private, emotionally charged meanings. Thus, "Why am I not heard?" "Because I am an angry, bad person and do not deserve to be heard." Or, "Why am I pushed out of center stage?" "Because I am exhibitionistic and rivalrous and want my mother to notice only me." Or, "I feel intruded upon, my boundaries violated." "But I bring it on myself because I enjoy the (sexual) penetration." These are not initially conscious and thought-through explanations, but among the patients who reported deficit phenomena (not being heard, not allowed to be the center of attention, being intruded on), these meanings (respectively, I am too angry, I am too exhibitionistic and rivalrous, my sexual wishes are at fault) were uncovered in the analytic process. Conflictual meanings get attached to experiences of deficit as they do to anything else. But one must be careful in looking through the analytic lens to see what is primary and what is secondary, or at least to see coexisting and complementary sets of forces. In the examples just given it seemed (over time and after trials of interpretation and noticing the responses to them) that the deficit experience—based on experienced lacks in the parental provision—was primary and the conflictual meanings were added on secondarily as "explanations."

The reverse also occurs, however: early conflict produces a situation where the child is later unable to receive what the parent has to offer and tries to offer. I am thinking of situations with children where early nonsatisfaction produces rage or withdrawal that makes the parent's later ministrations more feared, warded off, and embroiled in conflict. Such situations produce an ambiguity with respect to a "deficit" view: the supposed deficit in later care (which the adult patient may report) seems to be the result of the patient's own fearful withdrawal or hostility (as seen in the transference). The patient's experience is one of deficit, though during the analysis we come to see this as a result of yet earlier conflict that resulted in the child's warding off the parent. I believe this makes a difference in subsequent analytic work, though the starting point in the patient's subjective state may be similar.

Defects, too, can result from conflict. Thus, a child produces a pseudoimbecilic resolution of early conflict, drawing on stupidity as a way to preserve an otherwise taboo close link to the parents (Mahler, 1942; Pine, 1985). But that conflict solution produces effects, and in the child I saw, there were serious defects in learning and in the capacity to socialize beyond the parental webs; these defects followed her through her teens and into adulthood. In another example, early rage responses to a rejecting and emotionally destructive mother seemed to impair the development of object constancy; the very idea of the (remembered) object was regularly destroyed by rage and distrust (McDevitt, 1975).

Conflictual meanings can be added to defects, too, as unconsciously produced "explanations" of them—as I described earlier for deficits. Thus, a tendency toward emotional flooding (which in the particular patient I thought of as a defect based on early identifications with uncontrolled parental models) was "explained" by the patient himself: "This is just like wetting the bed; I can't control my urine or my emotions; something is wrong with my manliness." Or a neuropsychologically based difficulty in organizing the visual field was explained by the patient to himself: "I always used to peek into my mother's room; I deserve what I got as punishment."

My point with regard to defects and deficits, on the one hand, and conflict, on the other, is twofold. First, everything gets caught up in the inner system of wish, fantasy, and conflict; everything becomes a party to compromise formation. Defects and deficits are no exception. They are parts of intrapsychic life and as such subject to all the dynamic goings on of that intrapsychic life. In this sense, as I said at the outset, conflict is everywhere in the significant phenomena of any analysis. But second, defects and deficits have an existence of their own as well. They are residues of the developmental pathologies that are in addition to and yet interwoven with the conflict pathologies.

We do well to recognize the reality of deficits and defects in our own minds and at times to make this recognition explicit with a particular patient. I have found that failure to recognize the "raw wound" response to a deficit experience at moments in the analyses of particular patients is itself a repetition of the wound (Kohut, 1977, 1984). In addition, I have found that explicit recognition of either deficit experiences or defect phenomena can be extremely relieving and self-confirming to the patient in ways that permit the analytic work to move forward productively (although the acknowledgment of a defect also seems inevitably to produce humiliation or depression or hopelessness to some degree along with the relief).

There will always be interpretable conflictual meanings in any area of mental life, and these will enter into the transference. If one only waits, still another such interpretable conflictual meaning is sure to show up. Yet waiting for such meanings is sometimes a disservice to the patient, based on too much loyalty to a particular theory of technique or of psychopathology. Something else may be going on as well, and it may be one of the two phenomena I have defined as deficit and defect. It is in this sense that I suggested at the outset that, though conflict may be every*where* in mental life, it is not every*thing*. I do not propose a leap to the conclusion that this or that is deficit or defect early in an analysis. And I do not suggest that the view that something is a deficit experience or a defect in function rules out the role of conflict. But I do propose that we include in our thinking the differential diagnostic considerations put forth in this chapter even in the course of ordinary analytic work.

One brief aside before I conclude this chapter. I have noticed on a few occasions that capacities I came to view as "defective" (object constancy, affect control, and self-other differentiation in these particular instances) rather suddenly seemed to be present and functional in the patient in whom I thought of them as not available. Indeed, at these points, new conflictual meanings often emerged that seemed to "explain" the defect in function. But then, shortly, the function was seemingly absent again. How is one to understand this?

I am reminded of work with institutionalized infants reported by Provence and Lipton (1962). These infants were left virtually without human contact and seemed to lie in their cribs in a state of suspended animation, showing none of the age-appropriate developmental achievements that infants normally show, such as eye-hand coordination, the nonspecific smile, and so on. Yet the researchers, through active engagement with the infants, were able to elicit those behaviors at the appropriate time on the developmental timetable. The capacities were there, yet not there (as in my patients); they were functional when elicited but did not get used spontaneously. And they lapsed when the hard work of eliciting them ended. It would be worthwhile to consider whether some functional capacities are not either-or but are developed as potentials that are not reliably usable or still require stimulus nutriment from the outside (that is, a specific caretaker input) to make them work. The analytic setting may for moments provide this nutriment. Some such thinking seems to me potentially fruitful in understanding these particular now-you-see-it, now-you-don't clinical phenomena.

Last is the question of how to work with deficit and defect phenomena (each in its own way, since they are far from equivalent). For this I return to the distinction between conflict pathology and developmental pathology that I just alluded to (and see A. Freud, 1974, and Fonagy and Moran, 1991). Interpretation may be more fully suited to work in areas of conflict, though we well know that there is no one-to-one correlation between interpretation and insight or between insight and change. What I have tried to do in this chapter is to suggest that much *interpretive* work must be carried out in the developmentally faulted areas of deficit and defect as well. These phenomena may come into existence in part through conflict-ridden "solutions" and, in any event, are always secondarily involved in conflict, having fantasies ("meanings," "explanations") attached to them.

Work in these areas may also involve something more, however, something that includes description and explanatory reconstruction as well as the patient-specific efforts I have illustrated at points in this chapter. I am not saying that, in the area of developmental pathology, a caring object relationship is sufficient as the route to cure. While a benevolent atmosphere in the analytic situation will not hurt, and much good may often derive from it, the complex analytic task of interpretation and of finding other developmentally forwarding interactions and forms of intervention remains to be worked out in each instance—specific to the particular defect or area of deficit and to the patient's character and personality as a whole. This is not subject to rule-making with regard to technique. There is no substitute in any analysis for attentive listening, good-enough interventions, and making use of the clinical opportunities each patient offers to us. But only with a fully differentiated view of what in mental life is there to be changed can we hope to move ahead with our understanding of how analytic change takes place.

7 Clinical Considerations Regarding Interpretation in the Four Psychologies

Since 1985, when I published my first work on what I have come to call "the four psychologies of psychoanalysis," I have often been asked how one decides which psychology is active at the moment. How does one decide what and how to interpret? What are the guidelines determining the "choice" of interpretation in terms of the issues represented by one psychology rather than another? My response to all such questions is always the same: it all depends; I have no systematic guidelines outside the domain of my clinical listening. It depends on one's understanding of the patient in general and the clinical material of the moment. There is no other answer. That is the nature of clinical work. But the array of interpretive possibilities available to the clinician will be affected by the breadth of the conception of mind that is part of his or her inner working model. My aim in this chapter is to present several clinical instances in which I try to demonstrate the reasoning determining my decisions regarding intervention.

As in all clinical reasoning and all intervention decisions, different clinicians are likely to hear the material differently; that is, in fact, the premise of this entire book. But this does not mean that those various perceptions are random. Quite the reverse is usually the case, in that psychoanalytically oriented clinicians can usually readily recognize the clinical reasoning processes of others, even when the end point reached is quite different from their own.

In any event, I find that the task of arriving at a particular intervention is no different when working with a "four psychologies" model or within a single, seemingly more unified theory. The drive-defense model of the structural theory, for example, does not automatically provide interpretations flowing off the theoretical page. The question of interpreting at the oedipal or preoedipal level, interpreting in the transference or the outside life or the past life, interpreting in relation to the defense or the urge or conscience or all three—not to mention the questions of what to interpret and whether to interpret anything at all—are omnipresent. It is no different when working with multiple models. The material usually feels infinitely complex, and adding to the infinite still leaves us with infinite complexity, no more. Complexity is simply in the nature of the work. If theories of ego, object relations, and self have added understandings to those given to us by Freud's relatively more drive-based theories, then complexity—translated in this instance as difficulty for the clinician—is an irrelevant consideration. If we require multiple models or a more complex and many-sided overall model in order to hear patients adequately, then that is simply what the work entails, and it is the job of the clinician to master it as well as possible.

The current psychoanalytic theories see the mind as organized around different issues; or, to put it otherwise, they see different phenomena and conflicts as mattering most in psychic life. As I have said, I see these issues as additive rather than substitutive, new understandings rounding out our view of mind rather than replacing earlier understandings. Each of the "psychologies" is itself an internally complex conceptual view, with unresolved and sometimes internally contradictory ideas, with a broad reach to recognize (in its own terms) most of the issues addressed by the other psychologies, and with multiple versions of theory rather than a single monolithic set of ideas. Nonetheless, I will give a brief picture of the mind's issues as seen in the different theories. I have presented this in Chapter 2 in a somewhat different form, but I summarize the points here in a form that serves to introduce the clinical reasoning to be illustrated in this chapter.

From the standpoint of a psychology of *drive*, the individual is seen in terms of the vicissitudes of, and struggles with, lasting urges, most centrally and problematically sexuality and aggression. These urges are ultimately biologically based and unfold in a preprogrammed epigenetic sequence, but they achieve psychological representation and are subject to endless variation through the impact of experience. From the standpoint of a psychology of the *ego*, the individual is seen in terms of the gradual development of (or failures to develop) capacities for defense, adaptation, and reality testing, and the uses of these capacities in the clinical situation and in life to deal with the inner world of affects, urges, and fantasies and the outer world of reality demands. From the standpoint of a psychology of *object relations*, the individual is seen in terms of internal dramas derived from some combination of early object-related experiences and the fantasies and affects that determined how this early history was experienced and recorded in memory in the individual instance. These internal dramas, the internal images of past object relations *as experienced,* also put their stamp on new experience, so that these in turn are assimilated to the old dramas rather than experienced fully in their contemporary form. And finally, from the standpoint of a psychology of *self experience* (probably itself more a polyglot of theories than the others), the individual is seen in terms of an ongoing subjective state of self, particularly with regard to issues of boundaries, authenticity, agency, esteem, and affective tone.

In the clinical examples that follow, I address these several sets of issues *interpretively.* It is sometimes thought (erroneously, as I see it) that work in the different psychologies automatically entails basically different clinical approaches—perhaps interpretation in the drive psychology, some emphasis on "holding" and corrective object relationships in the object relations psychology, empathic mirroring in the particular aspect of a psychology of self experience that derives from Kohut's (1977) work, and perhaps something educative in ego psychology. None of that is what I am addressing here. On the one hand, any of these modes of intervention *may* enter into any treatment at some point, but it will enter in relation to the form and level of pathology at the moment and the place where one is in the particular analytic (or therapeutic) process; the modes of intervention other than interpretation are not inseparably tied to a particular view of mind. On the other hand, I conceive *all* the issues addressed by each of the psychologies to be relevant to the mental life of all persons, and I see interpretation as central to the analytic way of working with them. In Chapter 3 I addressed issues regarding the interplay of interpretive and relational effects in the therapeutic impact. That is not my focus here. I concentrate instead solely on the clinical reasoning underlying diverse interpretive interventions.

I give clinical material from four different patients in this chapter. In each instance I was supervising the clinical work or was a discussant at a conference where the case was presented. Each clinician was a trainee; the clinical work is basically sound but usually not highly sophisticated. (In the first two examples the clinician was a psychiatric resident conducting a twice-weekly psychotherapy; in the second two instances, the clinician was an analytic candidate conducting a four-times-per-week control analysis.) Because of the way in which the material was made available to me, I generally do not have follow-up sessions in which the ideas I put forth in the supervision or conference were tested. In only one instance (the second example given here) do I have such follow-up material. I offer here a few basic facts about each patient, process notes of particular sessions (from which I abstract the parts I wish to highlight), and my commentary. The commentary is meant to provide the clinical reasoning determining the basis for my recommendation that the interpretive work is misplaced and should have a different focus (*schematically,* that the interpretation should be in terms of a "different psychology"). I have not attempted to give patient histories or process notes in sufficient detail for the reader to make fully independent decisions about what is going on; my aim is to illustrate my own reasoning process, and I organize and abstract the material accordingly.

Not every session can or should be approached in terms of a possible shift from one psychology to another. The clinician should simply be listening, with all theoretical concepts well in the back of his or her mind. The sessions I give here were selected because they *can* be approached in this way. In each instance I heard the clinical material and discussed it. When it occurred to me that the material nicely illustrated the utility of thinking in terms of different issues of mind from the one the clinician was addressing, I would ask for a copy of the process notes for teaching and writing purposes. This opportunity does not come up often, but it is the basis for the particular case material offered here. This is a selection from among a large number of supervisory experiences in which these particular issues did not come up or were dealt with so automatically that they were not noticed.

The interpretive work I describe is the product of normal clinical listening, with evenly suspended attention. What attention is evenly suspended *over*—that is, the range of potential interpretive possibilities—is broad; I work with multiple models of mind. But I do not believe the work will seem so unusual to therapists. I suspect that the interventions I propose are part of the working array of interpretive possibilities drawn on by most therapists and analysts. Usually, while working, they have no particular interest in the question of whether the interpretations they offer are drawn from a single theoretical model or from many such models. Clinicians usually assume they have some kind of theory in mind and are bringing it to bear on the clinical material. But frequently, I believe, they are working close-up with whatever clinical material there is, irrespective of its place in a theory of mind. My aim here is to highlight the multiple-model thinking implicit in psychodynamic therapeutic work.

Some years ago, Sandler (1988), summarizing the papers presented at a meeting of the International Psychoanalytical Association, pointed out that most of the presenters conceptualized their cases in terms of drive-defense theory, but that most of the actual work centered around affects and object relationships. His aim was to show that therapists are not simply "applying" their theories to the clinical material (though they may think they are) but are responding close-up to the live clinical material at hand (which may or may not be organized around the issues of the analyst's preferred theory). My aim is a related one. While illustrating my clinical reasoning in suggesting interpretive shifts between different psychologies, I also intend to be illustrating clinical work that is probably not unfamiliar to most therapists who may practice it without awareness that they are working with multiple models of mind.

Example 1

A thirty-five-year-old female administrator, married and with one child, had been in twice-weekly psychotherapy for about eight months at the time of the two sessions to be described. She had originally entered treatment after an impulsive act on her part had thrown her into an emotional crisis. What happened was that she had slept with an old lover after an intensely angry argument with her husband. Soon after, she guiltily confessed it to him, and since that time both she and her husband had felt their marriage to be seriously ruptured. At the time of the initial presentation, the patient had seemed highly obsessional; her thought was a tangled mass of repetitive self-questioning, doubt, and tangential and ruminative thinking, all circling around on itself. But this pattern faded and, while it was not understood at this point in the treatment, seems to have been some sort of inner response to the impulsive act—self-doubting and self-paralyzing. At the time of the sessions to be reported, the patient had a strong attachment to her therapist, her thinking was reasonably clear and productive, and her marriage remained one of the major foci of the work.

The patient had had a psychologically (and sometimes physically) abusive past, usually at the hands of her mother. After her parents' divorce, however, when she was preadolescent, her father was virtually absent and was experienced as rejecting; the patient felt she had no choice but to accommodate, fearfully, to her mother's rantings and rages. She tried to please, to be good, to anticipate and meet her mother's every whim. She had come to understand that she also did this in the therapy and with her husband as well. At the time this understanding first developed, it seemed emotionally powerful.

On a particular Monday afternoon, the patient began by speaking, with considerable annoyance, about how her husband—"always indecisive," she said—demands her help in making each of his decisions. She resents this and feels terribly burdened by it, but she feels she has to pitch in and help him nonetheless. "Otherwise he might get angry." She feels she has to please him, to accommodate to him, in order to ward off that anger. "I guess I'm still afraid of being hit by 'Mommy,'" she said, readily recognizing the continuity with her old child self.

Then she got into what was, in the main, new material in the therapy. She told of how, before the divorce, her parents used to try to get her to take sides, to say who was right in the arguments between them, and of how frightened and burdened she felt by this responsibility because she knew she could only end up pleasing one parent and angering the other. But her mother "wasn't *only* angry and frightening," she now said for the first time; she was very gentle at times, teaching her daughter, the patient, how to cook and playing games with her. "It made it hard to want to leave her when she was her angry self" because she was so nice at other times, and the patient would feel guilty about her wish to run away.

"I had to be the good daughter," she added, "always trying to please. I still do that—with my boss, my friends, and still with my parents." And, the therapist added, "with Robert" (her husband). The patient saw that immediately and agreed.

I have radically foreshortened this session, to allow the main points I wish to discuss to stand out. At this juncture the patient was reasonably clear-thinking, able to make and hear connections, and even to bring forth new and significant material about the "good" mother. After I heard her report of the session, however, I learned something additional. I asked my supervisee what the patient's attitude and affect had been like in the session. The therapist's response was instantaneous: "Resignation," she said. Thus, though the patient sounded insightful (about how she fears her husband's anger and tries to ward it off by pleasing him, as she had done with her mother earlier), the real use of this "insight" currently was to confirm her sense that she was, through fear, guilt, and resultant efforts to please, hopelessly locked in the patterns of her past, hopelessly caught in what was now a repetition of an old, internalized object relationship, which she grafted onto each new situation, and, in this session, onto her relationship with her husband.

In the second session (presented to me in the same supervisory meeting), the patient came in two days later saying that she was angry at her husband and (once again) that she could not express her feelings to him, partly, she said, because of her sexual escapade: "He's looking for a reason to move out on me." But "he's so dependent on me," she immediately added. She thinks his dependency keeps him in the home. "But I wouldn't want to keep him dependent; I hate his dependency," she added. "But I think he will leave, and I don't want that."

The therapist, from all she had heard in the past eight months, had the sense that the possibility that this man would leave was virtually nil. So she commented simply: "You seem convinced he will leave." The patient responded in some detail, both confirming and questioning her belief. "Why am I so convinced he will leave?" she asked herself after her ruminations. Her therapist spoke: "I guess you're afraid you'll lose your father once more," again offering an interpretation based on repetition of earlier object relationships. The patient responded easily—too easily, I believe, because she was now using these "insights" into repetitive object relations defensively, as I shall shortly discuss—and she spoke of several childhood losses, telling how painful they were and how alone she felt.

Toward the end of the session, the patient came back to her brief sexual affair. "I was angry at him, so I did it. But now I'm afraid he'll leave me. So I have to accommodate to him again, and I hate that." To my question the therapist made it clear that the patient's attitude after this session continued to be resignation. The patient was feeling locked in her past, a past of fear, loss, and efforts to please in order to avoid these states. My impression was that "insight," once gained, was now being used as resistance. The patient's attitude was: "I see who I was; I see who I am. What can I do? I'm stuck." Her understanding of her repetition of the now-internalized old object relationships through pleasing and fear of anger and loss, a true step forward at an earlier point in the treatment, had turned to quicksand. She felt stuck, and the "insight" was being used to justify the situation.

Various points of interest might be discussed about these sessions, such as the emergence of her earlier ruminative tendency at a particular juncture and her rushing to another man at a moment of rage. I focus on one main idea: a shift in the "region" of interpretation into another "psychology." Again, I offer this not as a way to approach sessions systematically; I do not believe they should be so approached. Rather, I offer it for two paired reasons, both clinical: the patient's use of understanding about repetition seemed to be unproductive, indeed actively counterproductive, in these sessions, and other material seemed present and of potential significance.

On the basis of my impressions of this patient, formed in the previous months of supervision and through moments of interpretive work from earlier on, I suggested to the therapist three points where I thought interventions of a different sort could have been offered, with the intention of moving the process out of the stalemate it was in. The three are not equally compelling, but I give them here to illustrate the shift to formulation in terms of a different view of the issues in the patient's intrapsychic life. I describe them in descending order of my degree of conviction about them, starting with what seems clearest to me.

In the first session, the major thread had to do with the patient's sense that she always accommodates, always makes an effort to please.

"I guess I'm still afraid of being hit by 'Mommy'" was the way she summed it up. That is: I accommodate because I am afraid that otherwise I'll become the target of someone's anger, and I can't stand that. I suggested that the therapist might have said: "Yes, I believe you *are* afraid of being hit once again. But it's hard to believe you weren't also *angry* at your mother, and we *know* you are at Robert. So I suspect that accommodating, which began as your way of warding off your *mother*'s anger, has become your way of denying your *own.*" In other words (I add to the reader) what began as (and still is) an adaptive effort that became habitual—became, that is, a repetitive form of object relationship growing out of old strain trauma—has now been transformed and become also a reaction formation. "I am not an angry person; I am a pleaser." She accommodates not simply because of the unchangeable *past,* but as a means to undo and deny her own anger in the *present.*

A second possible intervention relates to material early in the second session. The patient, resentful of her husband's dependency, says the following (and I add a bit more from the process notes here): "I can't express my anger because I'm afraid he'll move out because of my affair. But he's really so dependent on me. I think it's his dependency that keeps him from leaving. But I wouldn't want to keep him dependent; I hate his dependency." Knowing from past work that this woman is also troubled by what she refers to as her own "neediness," I might respond as follows to her "I wouldn't want to keep him dependent; I hate his dependency" (which has a ring of "the lady doth protest too much"): "You say you don't want to keep him dependent, but you know how much your own 'neediness' troubles you, and how much you fear being left alone. I wonder if in fact you don't *keep* him dependent in subtle ways, by pleasing him so and helping him with all his decisions. That way you can feel *he*'s the needy one, not you, and yet keep him from leaving so you'll feel taken care of." What I have done here is to emphasize the patient's (probably marginally conscious) manipulation of her husband so that he depends on her; in so doing she externalizes the "dependency," the "neediness"—"it's him, not me." Again, I have chosen to focus on what she is actively doing in the present rather than "passively" repeating from the past, and again I have focused on her own rejected urges rather than the repetition of past object relationships.

And now a (possible) third intervention: the patient had ended her second session recalling her brief sexual affair. She said (and again I add a bit more from the process notes): "I was angry at him, so I did it. But now I'm afraid he'll leave me. So I have to accommodate to him again, and I hate that." I might have responded: "Yes, you feel you have to accommodate because of his anger at your evening with your old lover. But *you* were angry, too; that's a big part of why you did it, and your own anger frightens you. I wonder if your confession of your affair wasn't also designed to *provoke* Robert's anger. Then he's the angry one, not you, just like with your needy and dependent feelings." Then, after giving the patient time to respond, and if she seemed to be able to work with this idea, I might have added: "Another thing may be going on when you provoke his anger. You get to be in charge of when he's angry. You won't be as frightened if you can know when his anger is coming, if you are in control of it—something you once told me you wished you had been able to do with your mother, anticipate and control her anger." So, once again I have emphasized what the patient is *doing,* rather than what was *done to* her. I do this in part by showing her her inner struggles with her own anger, her attempt to make Robert the carrier of all of the anger.

I want to emphasize that the earlier work in the therapy, resulting in her ability to see how she repetitively reenacted her experience of her primary childhood object relations, had been valuable and a great step forward at the time. Now that understanding was being used to justify resignation, perhaps to cling to the past, perhaps to stay clear of any disruptive change or new insight. How could the resignation be dislodged? The resignation as a way of holding onto the past, as a form of attachment to the familiar-though-painful, could have been interpreted directly, though I suspect that the patient would have greeted that with similar resignation, an attitude of "What can I do, that's who I am." In the transference, the patient's repetition of the therapist's interpretation (about accommodation to avoid anger) could itself be interpreted as accommodation to, pleasing of, the therapist, and I think that would probably have had more impact, making the patient less content just to repeat the "insight," though perhaps still feeling resigned. But in these sessions I thought a vivid opportunity was presented to look at the clinical material in new ways—in terms of rejected urges and the defenses against them. The patient could be helped to see the way her "accommodation" and her resignation, residues of the past and her way of thinking about them, are being used to serve *present* functions—to disown her anger or neediness by placing it in Robert or, through being a "pleaser," to react against and disguise her present anger. Each of these had a potential transference manifestation in her effort to keep her neediness and anger out of her relation to her therapist. With this particular patient, these manifestations probably could have come into the work.

Why do all this? Because the mind is organized around many different issues, and each gets its turn in a full treatment. But the shift in focus comes up specifically at this juncture because of the patient's "resigned" use of the earlier insight into her enslavement in the repetitive object relations of the past. The understanding here of ego mechanisms, the understanding that the patient is now causing her own problems in large part, gives her responsibility for and ownership of her actions and her current life. That provides a basis for hope. If *I* did it, I can change it; if it were all done *to* me, I may or may not be able to affect it. The aim here is to enable the patient to move from seeing her role solely as victim of the past to seeing it also as perpetrator and perpetuator in the present.

Example 2
This second example involves interpretation in the domain of object relational or sexual issues and, in a second pair of sessions from work with the same patient, in the domain of object relations or the internal management of intense anger. This time the second session of each pair provides some follow-up.

The patient, a thirty-year-old male graduate student in history, one of three sons in a moderately estranged family, had been in therapy twice a week for about four years, having entered treatment in relation to inhibitions around sexuality. Shortly after beginning treatment with his female therapist, however, these inhibitions began to loosen up, apparently spontaneously, and the patient began to have sexual relations somewhat more freely. He would frequent singles bars, was interested in picking up women, and occasionally—though far from promiscuously—had sexual relations with them.

Much of the therapeutic work up to the point of the sessions I report had to do with his conflicted relationship to both parents. He was also very close to his mother in real-life ways, with strong gratification and equally strong disappointment in their ongoing contacts. She lived alone, and her son (the patient) spent many weekends at her home; he also had dinner with her frequently in midweek. Their relationship had never been satisfying. She was in the theater and traveled a lot, leaving her son as a child in the care of various governesses. The patient sought contact with her, and it was precious to him, even though he felt that she was an unreal, superficial person with values radically different from his own. He felt that she did not know who he was at all, had never really sensed what he was like. She could not understand (he said) why he wasn't more (if not quite in these words) superficial, showy, theatrical. He was too serious, too workaday, for her comprehension, and his graduate studies in history were proof of that for her. But the patient also felt that he had much of his mother in him.

The patient was completing his doctorate and moving to a university position in the coming autumn and now, some eight months before that time, the turn to a new calendar year brought his anticipated loss of his therapist into his awareness. There had been some talk about it in a prior session in which, additionally, a one-week vacation that the patient was planning was also discussed.

In the first of the two sessions to be described, which followed the session when the eventual ending of therapy and the patient's imminent vacation had come up, the patient came in saying he had been deeply moved by the prior session. He had tried to get work done on his thesis afterward, but realized he had to stay with his feelings for a while before he could even consider working. (This degree of ownership of painful feelings was unusual for him.) He then went on to speak of a recent visit with his mother. He again saw her life clearly, all full of show and wealth, saying that he did not want that; again she seemed unable to understand why he wasn't focused on marrying rich, being seen at the opera, or attending opening-night theater parties. The gap between them felt large to him but his involvement with her felt strong, as always.

Then he turned to discussing his vacation. He was going to Rio de Janeiro on his own, he said. He didn't know if he would enjoy it; he had made no real plans. But he loved seeing foreign countries, just walking the streets, looking at the people, going to the markets. He liked the little things, seeing the way people's lives are different from ours here, or just seeing the lights in a different city or the stop signs. These comments triggered a thought in the therapist's mind, although she said nothing. His sexual interests and frequenting of bars had previously connected for him with his ideas about Rio as a sexually free city. Now his reference to "walking the streets" and the "lights" and the "stop signs" made her wonder about his interest in *street-walkers* in the *red light* district—his sexual interest in Rio.

The patient went on: "Those things are so important to me, the little things, like the lights or the stop signs. Seeing that they are different from what we have here. [He starts to cry.] That's basically. . . . [He cries some more.] I don't know why it's hard to talk about these things. [He tries describing them again, but again he cries.] I just want to cry [and he does]."

The therapist spoke for the first time: "I'm not sure I understand what's making you so sad right now." The patient responded:

I don't know. It's just hard to talk. [pause] I just got an image of saying this to my mother. Like when I told her I was spending the weekend with a woman and couldn't visit her. She just won't accept something that is part of me that isn't part of her. That I have my own interests. I just don't feel comfortable talking to her about this even if it's a big part of my own life. It's silly, but I feel like crying. It's like there's something weird about me if I'm interested in the stoplights in another country. She wouldn't understand this. She'd only understand if I went there to hang out with some wealthy crowd and "do" the theater circuit. That's about it. In some ways I'm glad to have a more real type of life, but I don't feel it's all right to have that.

Soon after this, the therapist ended the session, which I have again radically shortened.

So, where might one have intervened—or was any intervention necessary? Let's start with the therapist's thought: walking the street and streetwalkers, lights and stop signs, and, later in the session, reference to stoplights—that is, red lights. In the language of primary process these are compelling associations. It may well be that something is going on in the realm of sexual fantasy; the patient's "made up" examples of the "little things" that interest him are suggestive enough to be considered from that standpoint. Perhaps a sexual issue is active.

But is that where the patient is in this session? I do not think so. He seems to be struggling with his relation to his mother and their divergent interests. That is what *he* says matters to him right now in the session—issues of object relation and self-other boundary—more specifically, the loss of connection to his mother if he is a different person from what she wishes him to be. Even the "little things" he emphasized are about how different people in different places are different from one another; his focus is on *his* acceptance and appreciation of difference, which he wishes his mother shared. The affect in the session is connected to this (his tears), and there is a sense of fit, of right timing, because this comes just before a separation from both his mother and his therapist, talked about in the prior session, in which the patient was "deeply moved." So perhaps no intervention is necessary because the patient sees this on his own. Or perhaps a remark that simply confirms what he sees, something like "It's painful to you to see the difference between the two of you." Or something that adds a bit to what he says in terms of his conflicting wishes: "You want so much to be different from her, and yet also to be close, and you wish she would help you with that so you needn't feel estranged as you go your own way." Whether this would be followed by reference to the transference, which was not primary in his associations, would depend on his response.

The sexual fantasy and his wishes may have entered in under the umbrella of this object relations focus. Thus, "It's not only the street lights or the theater that sets you apart from her, but your ideas about the sexual possibilities in Rio mean that once again you're 'spending a weekend' with another woman, and that too she wouldn't understand." Note that I have not interpreted anything about streetwalkers or red light districts; my sense is that those translations, even if correct, are too remote from the patient's consciousness and would take him too far from his deeply felt insights. On reflection, I would not have made even the intervention just suggested.

Can we imagine conditions under which the sexual issue (rather than the self-other boundary and object relationship issue) *would* have been the central one? Yes, but to illustrate that I have to invent a somewhat different session. I do that here to illustrate the clinical reasoning process.

Let us imagine that the patient had already, in a previous session, spoken of his fantasies of seeing prostitutes in Rio and about the guilt they provoked. He begins the current session as he in fact did, and then says something like this: "I keep thinking that all I want to do is walk the streets of Rio and see the lights and the stop signs. *I can't get that thought out of my head.* It's as though I'm justifying myself. I do like to just walk around in new countries and see the sights, but I don't know why stop signs or lights come to mind. And I keep thinking I'll tell that to my mother, and then feeling that I'd better not. But I know why that is. It's like we talked about last week; she can't stand my doing things differently from the way she would."

Here I might say: "How comforting to think that *she* wouldn't want you to be doing those things. But, as I recall your telling me last week, you yourself are both interested in the lights—the red light district, that is—and feeling guilty about going there. No wonder you're plagued with thoughts of both the lights and of signs saying 'stop'!"

In this imagined session I have moved interpretively squarely into the field of drive psychology: conflicts about sexuality, played out unconsciously and producing a new mini-symptom, the obsessional thought that he "can't get out of his head." Why would I move in this direction in this session? In sharp contrast to the actual session described earlier, here the link to his mother is trite, pulled out of his learned repertoire—not to explain, but to explain away the symptom (that is, I have imagined him saying that he knows why he cannot tell his mother his thoughts about seeing the lights and the stop signs, because she cannot stand his doing things differently). The affect of the real session (the tears) is nowhere to be seen in relation to the mother, separation, and separateness issues in the imagined session. In contrast, the affect is present in the obsessive quality of the thought that he "can't get out of his head." Whereas in the actual session my sense was that reference to the red light district would be too abstract, too conceptual, pulling him away from his vividly felt experience of his mother's intolerance for his individuality, here I would assume that the obsessive quality of the thought about lights and stop signs— their ego-alien symptomlike features—would have called the patient's attention to them and interested him in them enough so that he would be receptive to the interpretive translation and even relieved to find that sense could be made of his obsession.

These are all clinical considerations. There are no rules for when you interpret in one sphere or another. There is no substitute for clinical listening, clinical judgment. The clinician—not any rule— bears the responsibility for the choice of intervention.

Before leaving this example, I want to present the central thrust of the next (actual) session, though it does not bear on the question of which of the four psychologies to interpret in (although it confirms the object relational focus of the first session). The patient came back to the next session again quite moved by what had happened in the previous one (in which he had cried). Then he recounted a conversation with his mother. On the basis of that conversation he was now able to say: "I was acting like all I wanted to do was something sweet and innocent like look at lights while my mother would have me do all those phony things. But she started telling me all kinds of things to see in Rio, to walk around and see the sights and the interesting markets." The important thing, he felt, was that she was telling these things for him, so that he could enjoy himself. She really could see him, beyond herself.

In this description, it seems clear that, while the patient's conscious experience is now of being appreciated by his mother in his individuality, the sound of it is that his mother's pleasures and his own are not so far apart. She too spoke of the pleasures of walking around and seeing unusual sights. It may be the sense of *union* that his mother here gives him that permits his feelings of pleasure in her recognition of his *separate* life. I am reminded of something James Anthony (1970) wrote on the relationship between the parent and the (well-individuated) adult child: to their surprise, since they are unaware of the strength of identification processes, they often find they have a lot in common. That happened at this moment with this patient. His individual interests and his tie to his mother were suddenly unified.

I now return to my central aim in this chapter—to illustrate the clinical reasoning processes involved in interpreting in the terms of one or another of what I have called the four psychologies. It involves the same patient just discussed, in an additional pair of sessions on his return from his trip to Rio.

Some further history is needed in order for the reasoning about these two sessions to be understandable. The patient had, once in the first year of therapy and once in the third year with his current therapist, two mini-breakdowns, in each of which his capacity to function in his ordinary way seriously crumbled. (I need not describe the details of the nonfunctioning; I need emphasize only that they gave grounds for real concern about him.) The first incident revolved around a confusing and unsatisfactory sexual event with some women he had met in a bar, after which the patient began to feel panicky and disoriented. As the panic grew, he became aware of homicidal urges toward the women and then suicidal urges. He could not bear to be alone and went to the home of one of his brothers until a feeling of inner control returned, a process that took about forty-eight hours. The second incident occurred on a visit to his other brother's home during a holiday week. This brother had been depicted previously as dominating psychologically, riding roughshod over other people's feelings and wishes. The patient felt that he hardly existed as an entity for this brother. Toward the end of the visit, he became panicky—the content never became clear—and felt he had to leave his brother's home immediately. He fled impulsively, unable to complete his stay, and again experienced considerable disorientation and breakdown of his usual functioning. Now back to the current sessions.

In the first session on his return from Rio (the next after the one I just summarized briefly), he came in excitedly and spoke of his trip. "What an amazing surprise," he said. "When I got on the plane for the flight to Rio I met my old college roommate. He was going to Rio also, and we decided to spend the week together." It turned out, in the telling, that this roommate had been a close friend in the past and of considerable personal importance to the patient. He went on:

Basically the week was great—except for a couple of days when I had some problems. Actually, I thought I was going to have a breakdown or something. It was really bad. I was really de-pressed, but it only lasted a couple of days. What got me upset was that I didn't like the way Bill [the former roommate] was treating me. I don't know, I felt he didn't like me very much. It made me just so upset. I didn't realize how upset I was getting, and that made it even worse. Finally it was like I couldn't bear it any longer. I remember being in the hotel lobby and having all I could do to keep from just smashing something. I wanted to put my fist through something, anything, anyone. In my room later—I had brought along a copy of one of the chapters of my thesis—I just tore it into shreds; I had to destroy something. I just wanted to cry. I felt like running off somewhere, but I was afraid to be alone, afraid I'd really go crazy if I were alone. I don't know what happened; somehow I got started watching TV. I tried to use it to calm me down, and it helped, slowly. I felt really dependent on Bill. I had to have his attention. I stayed in his room a lot of the time so as not to be alone.

I suppose I should try to understand why it all happened, like my past or something, but maybe that's not so important. I felt I couldn't do even the simplest things . . . but the TV helped. At least I could pay attention to that. That was reassuring. I'm afraid if I just dwell on that mood I won't be able to get out of it again. Or maybe I can figure it out so I won't get so upset next time.

The therapist spoke: "It would be useful to try to figure out what happened. You said you didn't like the way Bill was treating you?"

The patient replied: "I felt he didn't really like me, like he wasn't paying any attention to me. Bill met a bunch of his friends down there; that's why he was going to Rio. He spent a lot of time with them, but he invited me along. But I felt he really liked them, not me, that he'd prefer spending time with them. We all went to a party together, but Bill went off for a while with some of his friends. I felt really left out, like no one liked me. It was after that that I started getting depressed. I felt really alone. I don't think he even noticed that I was depressed." He went on to some further details. After a while he spoke of how he had displayed his depression and anxiety until Bill finally noticed him and tried to be helpful. It seemed clear to the therapist that Bill was essentially friendly throughout, though torn between the patient and the group of friends he had gone to meet; the patient himself seemed to realize that at this point.

The therapist, somewhat at a loss, yet wanting to help make sense of things and struck by the patient's *display* of his troubled state to Bill, said: "You know, I'm reminded of that time when you were a child and something had made you very unhappy, and you tried to hold onto the unhappiness until your mother noticed it and could show she cared about you." The patient's response was lukewarm. "I know the two times sound alike. But I felt nothing I could do would reach Bill. That's not like my mother. She loved me too much; I couldn't ever get away from it. In Rio, I started really feeling rotten about myself. I thought no one could like me."

The therapist, trying again, and now drawing on the issues of loss that had "deeply moved" the patient before his vacation trip, said: "Perhaps this is not so mysterious. You've had a lot of separations and losses in your life, and now you felt it was happening with Bill as well."

The session went on for a while longer, but I have summarized the essence of it as I saw it. I thought what the therapist had said was not unreasonable, especially in light of the recent separation from her for the vacation and the anticipated loss when he left therapy for his new university position. But I also think the therapist was unduly influenced by the supervisory sessions prior to the vacation, and in the present instance, it just did not seem to me that the partial object loss (of Bill) was of sufficient moment to account for the intensity of the patient's reaction. The patient, trying to be cooperative with the therapist, who mattered greatly to him, nonetheless gave a weak reply, neither convincing nor convinced. That is, the interpretation in terms of the triggering effect of object loss—an interpretation within an object relations psychology—went nowhere.

In the supervisory session I discussed the following points: that nothing we knew of his history fit with the idea that an object loss, a rejection, would trigger such disorganization; that the object loss intuitively did not seem important enough; and that the two prior experiences of disorganization did not have loss as a central feature. But my ear was caught by his rage—his feeling that he had to destroy something, that he was impelled to put his fist through something, his tearing his thesis chapter to shreds. My sense was that his ego-dystonic anger was of sufficient power to produce the disorganization that we were hearing about.

In addition, and I discussed this with his therapist, my supervisee, the history of two "breakdowns" (that we knew of—perhaps there were more) also called attention to his intense anger. In the first breakdown also, he reported both homicidal and suicidal impulses. The second one was less clear; his brother was described in ways that made anger, even intense anger, seem a likely response to him, but we had not heard that directly from the patient.

There was one other consideration operative here that was not simply a matter of listening to the patient in the current session and trying to work closely with wherever he was—normally the best way of working. That was my wish to have his therapist move with him into the heart of the "breakdown" experience before his therapy with her ended. The patient had done good work with this therapist, and she with him. Might the Rio events provide access to this experience? My own sense from the patient's words in this session, as noted, was that rage could have been the trigger to the psychological collapse. Perhaps the stimulus to his rage with Bill was the patient's feeling of being left out; but it seemed to me that the rage, once active, was what got out of hand and touched off the collapse. In any case, given the real basis for concern about these periods of psychological collapse, and given that we had another one recently at hand, I wanted to see whether the therapist could seize the opportunity to enter into them.

I probably would have said little more to the patient, as a starter, than "Can you tell me more about that feeling that you just wanted to destroy something?" Where I went from there would depend on the patient's response. If he responded in ways that permitted it, I might have gone on to inquire about rage in the other two "breakdowns," perhaps even ending with some formulation about how his anger, once triggered, frightens him into the falling-apart state, thus attempting to enhance his ego control processes. The emphasis on the aggressive impulses and failed defense against them leading to impaired ego function—that is, drive-defense issues rather than object relational ones—is based solely on clinical judgments made at the time. I have given the basis for the judgments I made, and I told all this to my supervisee.

In the next session the patient came in, said he had something on his mind, and did not want to continue with the issues of the prior session. A friend of his had been diagnosed with leukemia, and he wanted to talk about that. And that is what he did. But the following session saw a reopening of the material just discussed. The therapist was somewhat leading into the anger, and probably brought it in too early, being clearly interested in it after my comments in supervision; but what opened up in the patient seemed thoroughly genuine, as well as surprisingly intense and wide-ranging.

The patient started out by saying that he was spending a lot of time at home, not going out at all. (This withdrawing from life characterized the period following the first collapse as well.) Then he spoke of expecting his mother to visit, and how he anticipated being uncomfortable because she did not understand him at all. Here the therapist introduced the idea of anger, suggesting that his mother's not understanding him might make him angry as well as "uncomfortable." But the patient reemphasized the discomfort, and added that when he was uncomfortable he got to feeling nervous and dependent. The therapist tried again: "I was thinking of those other times when you got dependent, like when you were upset in Rio and had to stay near Bill. I wonder whether you felt angry when Bill was with his other friends, and whether it's that anger that makes you feel uncomfortable and then needy."

This freed the patient astonishingly and led to a flood of insightful self-description about his experience of anger and his conflicts with it. These were new communications in the therapy. They had not been expressed in any way before. I give only the barest summary of what he said.

To the therapist's comment, he immediately went further into the Rio story. He *was* angry, *very* angry, when Bill was with his other friends. But he also felt that he couldn't say anything about it, that his anger wasn't justified. After all, Bill had every right to be with his

friends; he had gone to Rio in order to be with them. "But I specifically remember telling myself that there was no reason to feel as angry
as I was getting. I couldn't just tell them to stop spending time together. I couldn't say anything at all to them about it. To do so would
have been to embarrass myself, to make myself look horrible." He
went on in some detail about the events, ending with: "I can't say
anything, but I just get nervous and uncomfortable and dependent. I
get afraid I'm going to do something *terrible.*" Therapist: "Like when
you felt like smashing your fist through something." Patient: "Right!"
Then *he* spontaneously went to the first breakdown. "Like that time
when things went wrong with those women and I felt like killing that
other person or myself." He went on to talk about how dependent
he became that time, but how he felt a lot better at another occasion when he told the other people involved to just "fuck off." Then
he went directly into another rage situation, one the therapist had
known nothing about, but where the patient had for some reason felt
entitled to his rage and did not go through any psychological collapse
as a result of it (similar to the "fuck off" incident).

The therapist returned to the earlier theme of the session. "Does
that anger ever come with your mother? Is it unthinkable with her?"
This time the patient spoke of feelings parallel to those he felt in Rio:
he was unjustified; he would do something terrible. He said, among
other things: "She's so fragile; I can't imagine saying mean things to
her. What would I do? Punch her in the face and say I was sorry?"

Perhaps this is enough to give the sense of the session, which continued in this vein. It was clear that the therapist's attention to the patient's anger had a freeing effect and took the therapist and patient
right inside the workings of his collapses. That is, anger and feeling
that he had "no right" to feel it or express it produce the urge to do
"something terrible" and the fear of doing just that, and then in turn
the feelings of being "uncomfortable, nervous, and dependent"—feelings that *are* the phenomena of the breakdown as he experiences it.

This is ordinary clinical work (although in the instance of these last
two sessions it paved the way for important changes in the patient).

We listen and we try to locate the significant way in which the material is active and organized in the patient's mind at the current moment. But sometimes these ways are differentially central in one or another theory, one or another view of how mind is organized. In the first pair of sessions, object connection, boundaries, and differentiation were at the center, though the therapist had tentatively been thinking in terms of sexual conflict. In the second pair of sessions, the therapist continued to think in object terms, now around object loss and separation, though the patient truly opened up insightfully and constructively when attention focused on his unintegrated rage. Same patient, different sessions, just a vacation week apart. All the issues come up in one way or another in all patients.

Example 3

The patient, a twenty-two-year-old woman living at home with her parents, had sought treatment because of a long history of difficulties in intellectual work—first notably in high school but now affecting her work at her local community college—and a more recent awareness of difficulties in relationships, particularly, she thought, with female friends, friends who were important to her but whom she felt on the verge of alienating.[1] She had come once a week for about a year and a half and then agreed to enter an analysis four times a week with her therapist, a candidate at an analytic institute. The session discussed here took place about five months into the analytic portion of the treatment. It revolved around the sequelae of a disturbing event about two months before that had preoccupied her and kept her angry ever since.

The material was presented to me in a clinical conference where, by my request, the history was given very briefly so that the focus could be on the process notes of a session selected by the treating analyst. In that brief history the presenter chose to mention one childhood event that stood out for him in the patient's recital of her history in the early

---

1. I want to express my appreciation to Jeremy Darnel, Ph.D., for allowing me to use this material.

sessions. "I came home from school one day really flying high. I was elated. I had just learned that I had gotten the highest grades in my class in my PSATS [the precollege board tests]. It was the one time I felt my anxieties about learning didn't get in my way! But when I walked into the house with my news, my mother was depressed as usual. She was just sitting there stroking her cat. She didn't even look up at me. I sunk inside." A second point the analyst chose to mention in his brief summary of the background to the session was that in her first session on the couch when the analysis itself began, he chose to be moderately active, to give her an ongoing sense of his presence, since he was now out of her line of vision. He did this, he said, because he somehow got the feeling that the nonresponsivity of the patient's mother and the patient's wish and need to be sure she was being heard and responded to were in the air. I hardly think it was accidental that the analyst chose to report those two facts before beginning the report of the session, though, strikingly, he did not make use of them in his understanding of the session. I believe he knew something preconsciously that he did not yet have words for, or that did not have sufficient centrality in the theory he was silently carrying inside as he conducted this analysis.

The event from two months earlier that the patient was still coping with in this session was an end-of-semester, pre-Christmas party that was given by one of her professors at his home. She had gotten seriously drunk at the party. Later that night, when friends were driving her home, she gathered from what they were saying that she had been seen in the garage with a classmate, Lawrence, with her clothes unfastened and half removed. She had no recollection of this, though she did not doubt that her friends were speaking the truth. She immediately felt a shudder of anger and humiliation with a sense of having been used and exposed by Lawrence. In the days immediately after, she thought she noticed this or that symptom and underwent a series of tests for sexually transmitted diseases; this added to her sense of humiliation.

The patient had been enraged at Lawrence ever since. She confronted him and demanded that he acknowledge what he did and apologize, but he refused to do either. She even telephoned and left a long message about what had happened on his parents' home answering machine, pleading with them to do something about it. But she never heard a word; they had not even, she said, bothered to call her back. Still extremely upset, she spoke about it to her parents, and each in turn failed to give her a response that satisfied her. Her father, a minister, and a man who always denied feelings and anything discomforting, urged her to "forgive" Lawrence in her mind. Her mother, angry and judgmental when not depressed, said it was the patient's own fault: she shouldn't have gotten drunk. Through all this, the patient has felt unable to "let go of" her anger. She has said several times, in fact, that she doesn't want to let go of it. In this session, she reports that her good friend Alice, one of the few friends she is not afraid of having alienated, has also spoken of the patient's "not letting go of" her anger.

The patient came in to her session saying it was a beautiful day, that it was hard to have a bad day on a day like this. She was tempted to just take the day off and spend it outdoors, but she couldn't let herself jeopardize her school grades. "I had lunch at school with Alice and we were talking about my doctor visits. I hate going. These tests for STDs [sexually transmitted diseases] are humiliating. And this is all because of Lawrence. I have one more test to do—for HIV. I keep putting it off. The whole idea upsets me. But Alice said she would go with me. I'll probably take her up on it and ask her to come. I had wanted someone to come with me because I'm so bothered by the reason I am there. I told Alice that it's going to be one of my worst days ever when I go, and she said, 'You've had your share.'"

"We also talked about grudges. I usually forgive . . . but not with Lawrence. I can't begin to consider forgiving. He didn't even admit he was wrong. Why should I forgive him!"

At this point the analyst commented that she had brought this (forgiving) up before, that it is like a debate she conducts with herself. The patient immediately added,

I think about it all the time. It's like Dad's sermons in church—to forgive. Would John Kennedy forgive Lee Harvey Oswald if he had survived those shots? I wonder what I'd do if Lawrence asked me for forgiveness. I don't want him to ask because I don't want to forgive him. But it does make it hard for me, this hanging on to my anger. I can't come to terms with it. But I don't want to let it go either. A couple of weeks ago I passed the Catholic church; I know Lawrence goes there. I had this fantasy that I would go inside, see Lawrence going into the confession box to seek absolution, and that I would sneak up and scream to the priest that he doesn't deserve forgiveness, that he's a cowardly, sneaky animal. I never before felt such hate in my life. . . . Alice is totally surprised by all this. She thinks I've taken all the anger I would have at everyone and anyone and directed it all at Lawrence.

Analyst (picking up on Alice's reported comment to introduce a theme, displacement of anger, that he stays with through questions and interpretations): "So Alice says that Lawrence is like a lightning rod; he draws all your anger." Patient: "Yeah . . . I never before felt such hate. I can accept hate for him." Analyst: "So perhaps if you're not careful, if you let your guard down, you'll discover such hate for someone else." The patient responded:

I can't think of anybody I would hate like that. Maybe there are other sources of anger that I blame on Lawrence. I got upset with my older brother recently and said—silently to myself—that I hated him. But I didn't really hate him. It was just frustration and anger, and it passed. I am confused about really *hating.* You know, it has to do with my father I guess, and his being a minister. Like sex or drugs—they don't seem to be such a big deal. I don't bring religion into them. I don't worry very much about the rules of the church and how one is supposed to live. But hate and forgiveness, they seem like pretty big deals, pretty basic. . . . But maybe it's still too soon after what Lawrence did. It's only a couple of months. But, you know, I don't even find myself moving in that direction. I *want* to hang on to this. It's an easy outlet for my anger, my sadness. And sometimes it's probably real.

Analyst (again thinking in terms of some defensive function of the anger at Lawrence): "I wonder if something makes you avoid a search for other sources of your anger" (the lightning rod theory). Patient: "Other things seem trivial by comparison." Analyst: "For example?" Patient: "Like exhaustion from being so busy. But that's not a reason for my degree of upset. Others would say that's not important enough." Analyst: "So there's no place for the little wounds. It's got to be gaping."

The patient again responds, but to the idea of a gaping wound: "Yeah, that explains why I won't let this wound heal. And so much is unresolved. I got no response from my phone call to his parents. I've never gotten to express my anger at him. It's a problem of being undeserving of my feelings, unentitled—or at least that's how I think *others* feel." Analyst: "Others?" Patient: "Like Mom for sure. She said long ago to just let it go. Even I wonder if these feelings about Lawrence are justifiable. Like I say to myself, 'You got too drunk; forget it.' But on other days it sounds like the *worst* thing. What am I supposed to think and feel? My friend Charlie suggested I get legal help. That influenced my whole response. But at least Charlie let me be upset. Maybe that's a good thing. So much of how I feel comes from other people's responses, affirming or not affirming. [Long pause.] I think in a way it's good that my friends took it all very seriously, or *I* wouldn't have. Just the fact that his parents didn't respond makes me angry. They must not take me seriously." Analyst: "Do you think they might be ashamed?" Patient: "Maybe. But my response if I were them would be to want to say *something*." And the session ends.

As I have pointed out along the way, the analyst is working with the idea that the patient's rage at Lawrence is serving a defensive-expressive function; that is, it both releases whatever other angers are stored up in relation to her whole inner self and history and obscures the true sources of those other angers by refocusing them on to Lawrence. He does this with his "lightning rod" phrasing, his comment that she is wary about letting her guard down lest she discover hatred of others, and his comment about her wishing to avoid knowing about other sources of her anger. The patient is not unwilling to try out these ideas, but she does so only a bit, giving them little more than lip service. They do not really take hold for her. Her comments, as I hear them, do not have the ring of a defensive flight from the displacement-defense interpretations; those interpretations just do not connect with her. More than that, I think, they are themselves potentially part of the problem, as I shall describe, though they do not seem to have become that clearly in the reported session.

I do not see this session as best understood in terms of drive-defense conceptions of mind. Rather I believe (and unfortunately I have no follow-up on this; the session was already an old one when it was presented to me) that the session is about narcissistic mortification and rage and a strengthening of the "self" by holding onto the anger, both of these in the context of the wish or need to be acknowledged. That context of acknowledgment explains why the analyst told me (at the conference) about the power of the mother's nonresponse in the background story of the history and about his sense that the patient needed a response from him in the first session when she was on the couch.

The patient tells the story of the session in terms of who does and who does not acknowledge her. Lawrence does not. His parents do not. Her parents do not, though each is motivated differently (religiously or blamefully). And, though it is unsaid, and the patient does not seem to me to be angry at her analyst, by the very act of interpreting the displacement, the analyst is not acknowledging the patient's sense of "justice" in her anger. I believe her anger is serving to counteract the mortification of having been used sexually and having been seen by others in the act. She is directly expressing her rage at its prime target, Lawrence, as well as for not being adequately (in her terms) responded to by the people closest to the event. (We of course do not know the actual event; I am addressing what I see as the patient's subjective experience of it and her current subjective state.) It may be that she is not angry at the analyst because he has acknowledged that anger sufficiently in earlier sessions since the event— perhaps repetitively, perhaps so much so that in this session he is trying to see it differently in order to get her unstuck.

In the fantasy that the patient creates regarding Lawrence's seeking absolution for his "sin," she responds ragefully. It is, I believe, too little too late; her rage still requires finding its target.

The patient also describes those who *do* hear and acknowledge her. Alice says, "You've had your share [of bad days]" when the patient is speaking of the bad day coming up. And she says of Charlie, who took her seriously enough to suggest that she get legal help, that "at least he let me be upset. Maybe that's a good thing." And "it's good that my friends took it all very seriously." That enabled her to do so, she says, in spite of the fact that Lawrence's parents (like her own) did not respond as she wished them to. When the analyst responds to this last exchange in the session by wondering whether the nonresponse from Lawrence's parents is due to their being ashamed, I believe he again risks undercutting the patient's sense of justice in her anger. But her response is to stick to her guns and maintain her anger.

It is easy to see the session in these terms if one's theory of mind has a place in it for the centrality of narcissistic rage and the (at least temporary) self-preservative function of anger, a place equal to that for a theory of mind organized around drive, defense, and compromise formation, or around the repetition of internalized object relations, or whatever. For this patient, in this session, I believe that is where the psychological aliveness is. This is a patient who, we are told, has one piece of history that lodged most indelibly in the analyst's mind: her nonacknowledgment by her mother—not, in that instance, nonacknowledgment of her anger, but nonacknowledgment all the same. How the two go together remains to be understood.

It would have been useful for the analyst to underline that the patient felt justified in her rage and that it strengthened her in the face of the insult she allowed herself to fall into. Or it could have been pointed out that those who take her anger seriously seem to give her the strength to take it seriously herself, while those who fail to do so themselves become targets of her anger, but an anger different in degree from the one she feels toward Lawrence. But I do not believe the work would end there. There are many directions in which it could go, though that cannot be foreseen. It might go in the direction of a general propensity toward narcissistic rage, although it need not, considering that this rapelike experience may have had enough distinctive traumatic force to cause an exception to her ordinary mode of response. Or the work might go toward the history of nonacknowledgment by the mother and *its* possible generality in the mother-daughter relationship and impact on her character and functioning (a "raw wound"). Or the work might go toward the lightning-rod-displacement-defense idea, which may turn out to have a validity that underlay the analyst's choice to move in that direction in this session but that I, an outsider to the treatment, do not know about. But my main point is, first things first. And in this session it is the patient's self-recognized wish or need not to "let go of" the rage at Lawrence that has center stage and is the appropriate starting place for the analytic work—perhaps around its current function for her, possibly with transference manifestations as well, perhaps additionally around its place in her history, but overall around its place in her "personal psychology."

Example 4

The patient, a fifty-five-year-old widowed schoolteacher, sought analysis when the birth of her first grandchild precipitated the recurrence of some painful symptoms that had been dormant several years, following a long history in adolescence and young adulthood when they had been crippling.[2] She found herself afraid that she might drop or drown or otherwise injure her granddaughter when she was caring

---

2. I want to express my appreciation to Barry Braskey for allowing me to use this material.

for her. These thoughts (not impulses, she emphasized, just thoughts) plagued her sufficiently that she found herself avoiding the very babysitting that had been giving her enormous pleasure; her fear was that she would do actual harm to her grandchild.

This symptom seemed to be a direct continuation of what had been present earlier. When she was a counselor at a summer camp in her late teens, she developed the fear that, on a day hike when she built a campfire, she would ignite a forest fire and cause multiple deaths; she resigned her job in midsummer on a pretext because of the extent of her fear. When she began to teach a kindergarten class, she grew fearful when she handed out scissors during artwork, again with the idea that she would accidentally poke some child with one and do serious damage; she managed to contain that fear and not leave her job, though the idea tormented her. When her own son was born, she had had fears similar to those she was now having with respect to his daughter. Many instances of similar obsessions often led to serious inhibition or renunciation to avoid what she felt was the danger of losing control and causing harm.

A central fact of her history was that her father, a World War II veteran who had participated in island-hopping invasions in the Pacific war against the Japanese, apparently suffered a long-lasting traumatic war neurosis which he insisted on keeping secret (within the family) and so never sought outside help for it. Nor did he ever discuss it with his only child, the current patient; only in her adulthood did she come to understand anything about his history. The central thread of her childhood memories was of hearing nightmarish screams and thrashing sounds from her parents' bedroom in the middle of the night. She feared, at various times in her childhood, that her father was killing her mother or some intruder, or getting ready to come and kill her. There is external confirmation for the father's nighttime screams, which went on at least through her teens but occasionally also at least until she left home after college. She became terrified of any and all anger; she tried to be good, to be well controlled. It was in this historical context that her symptom erupted.

In the first year and a half of the treatment, prior to the time I heard about the patient at a conference, the central thrust of the interpretive work had taken shape around the patient's own anger, her inhibition of it, and its displacement into fears of harmful action. Father's night awakenings with murderous-sounding shouts and thrashing about were seen as the model for dangerous loss of control; it was what would happen to her if she did not stay in control of her anger.

Four sessions, a week of analytic work, were presented to me at the conference. As before, I give the process notes selectively by quoting, summarizing, and skipping at various points. The sessions form a unity of sorts, the patient circling back in the fourth session to a dream from the first—having, in a sense, unconsciously filled in the details in the sessions in between. I try to show that, as I understand the material, the patient has turned to issues of connection to her father and to related issues of self-definition—not in terms of boundaries but in terms of self-worth, of "being an interesting person"— while the analyst is still hearing the material in terms of defense against anger. As in each of my other examples, I do not mean to suggest that the main interpretive thrust of the work to date had been in error: quite the reverse, in fact. I believe it had been central and would again become so; but now the patient was bringing in other aspects of herself. Think of this as reflecting overdetermination or multiple function, or as going to other "levels" of her functioning; or think of it, in terms of multiple models, as reflecting other issues of mind that were now achieving centrality in the analytic work.

The patient had recently returned from a vacation trip to Mardi Gras in New Orleans and had the previous week been speaking of the elaborate costumes she saw on the streets there. In the first session of the next week, she recounted a long dream, in which "I was back in New Orleans. The streets were crowded with people. I saw blood streaming down someone's arms. I wasn't afraid. I thought to myself: 'Oh, that's just part of the costume.'" In the session, in relation to some other material, the analyst made one or two interventions on the theme of inhibition of aggression but not much was done with the dream in this session.

To give a sample of the ongoing work, let me present a few moments from the second session of the week. I do not aim for any sort of continuity or completeness, just a sampling. Analyst (after a while in the session): "What were you thinking when you spoke about feeling isolated from your co-workers but also fearing getting too close?" Patient: "I fear that if people know me, they won't like me. And what if I get close to people and start getting my fears, like that I might hurt someone, or say something nasty about them behind their back? I don't want to get into that. So I keep my distance." Analyst (later in the session): "Certain thoughts seem dangerous to you; there are parts of your mind you don't feel free to explore." Patient: "Yes, and if I allowed myself to be fully engaged, I might embarrass myself. I might be dangerous to someone or hurt their feelings." Patient (still later): "I just remembered something. The doormen in my building often bring up any packages that get delivered rather than just leaving them at the concierge desk downstairs. So yesterday one of them did that. But the package looked slightly torn, and I got obsessed by the idea that he had been starting to open it to find out what was inside. I commented to him that the wrapping was torn, and I think he felt accused. I felt weird about that." Analyst: "Weird? Also angry?" Patient: "Yes, I was angry. I thought of telling the building superintendent. But that put me into conflict." Analyst: "So you feel caught between trying to protect yourself from injury and fearing that you'll hurt someone else." Patient: "Yes. That's familiar."

I want to give more detailed attention to the third session of the week, when something new and different began to come into the session. Something about the analyst's demeanor touched off a thought in the patient about illness and loss. This led her directly to her now quite old father and her fears of losing him before long. And this in turn led to some memories of a conversation at a recent visit to her parents' home. Patient: "We had some conversations. It was odd how much he and I agreed on things. I told him I was starting to try to learn how to cook some new dishes. Mom said it was easier to just get things like those at the gourmet shops in New York, or even frozen and packaged. But I said it's fun to make things from scratch, and Dad said that he agreed. As I told this to my son, I felt this connection to my father. I haven't been able to feel that for a long time. I think I don't like to see any part of myself as being like him. I'm afraid I'll become like him, start having screaming and thrashing fits in the middle of the night. Probably that's in my imagination, but I used to fear it would really happen. If I felt weird before going to bed, I would see it as a sign that something was going to happen." Analyst: "So you scan inside to see if something is wrong with you." Patient: "Yes. I always do that." Analyst: "It must make feelings all the more threatening. If you feel any anger, then you're like your father. Feelings always mean more than what they are."

My sense here is that the analyst has turned the session back into the familiar theme: the patient's self-scrutinizing and wary defensiveness against any sign of anger, any sign of being like her father. The patient's story of being *like* her father in a pleasing way, around the cooking, of feeling close to him, and her concern about losing him as he gets older, were left unaddressed at this point.

The patient, following the analyst's last reported intervention ("If you feel any anger, then you're like your father. Feelings always mean more than what they are"), said: "That's true. Something can't just happen. It foretells something else. [pause] I found as you said that [about anger, like her father] that I started not to listen. Your voice went to the background, and something else came to the foreground. [And here she tells a brief story of another incident at work where she was careful to be 'fair,' not hurtful. And then she continues.] But I'm wondering why I let that in my mind when you were saying something. It was weird, almost like my walking away from the place where your voice was and leaving you in the distance." Analyst: "Was there something you didn't want to hear me say?" Patient: "I was afraid that you would give me a reasonable explanation. I didn't want you to explain things. . . . I didn't want to hear something that sounded so rational. . . . I'm trying to understand why I blocked out your voice. Maybe it's something I didn't want to lose. Why would that be? There *are* things I see as a symptom of something larger, and I don't want them reduced to something that happens to other people." Analyst: "If these were just things that happened to other people, how would you feel?" Patient: "Sort of foolish. The patterns have gone on so long. Or maybe I'd feel like just an ordinary person. I'm thinking how many times I wish I were just a normal person [she means, without her fears of causing injury]. On the other hand, it's what I'm afraid of being. . . . If I feel confused, in part that makes me feel there is something different inside me, though it's not directed in a productive way." Analyst: "Feeling confused makes you feel there is something special inside, different from others, not ordinary." Patient: "Yes! Not positive different. But still different somehow. As I said that, I'm thinking that nothing I've said makes sense. I've been letting my mind wander. Like the other day when I talked about the dream and I said there was something else but I didn't know what" (a reference, I believe, to the bloody Mardi Gras costume dream, which is yet to return in the next session).

Here, I believe, the patient has introduced two new ideas, though neither she nor the analyst yet has recognition of them. (I say this partly on the basis of events still to come in this session, but also on the basis of the patient's fading the analyst's voice out. Also, her doing and undoing—that she is not ordinary and not making sense—suggest the possibility that something new is both emerging and being retracted.) Could it be that her "symptom" has also become a way to give herself value, something that makes her different from "ordinary" people, something she "doesn't want to lose"? In addition, does she not want to lose the tie she was feeling to her father—not, now, a tie based on her fear of being out of control like him, but of having something good in common with him? She said she did not want to hear what the analyst would say, did not want to lose something, did not want it reduced to something that happens to other people. Perhaps the analyst *was* reducing it. Not that the interpretations about defense against anger and feared identification with the father were off the mark in the past; they seem to have been important in the development of the analysis, and they clearly make sense, given the family history and the symptom history. But to bring them in now in this session may be "reducing" the patient, "taking something away." She did not want her closeness to her father to be reduced to a fear of being out of control like him, but to include love of cooking; she did not want her symptom history to be seen just as illness, but as making her into a very special, an interesting, person.

However, the analyst is trapped in a drive-defense view of the patient's functioning and does not see the object-connection and identity issues at this moment. And so, after the patient has said the things just reviewed but followed them by saying she is not making "sense," the analyst says: "What does make sense to me is that there are times when you are vigilant to see if there is evidence that there is something wrong. You fear that you might become like your father. And there are other times that you need to remain confused and not look at or know yourself." (But the patient had just said: "If I feel confused, in part that makes me feel there is something different inside me, though it's not directed in a productive way.")

Near the end of the session the patient recalled something she had done in the early morning that very day, and a dream from the night before. "I started doing all sorts of little things this morning. I read the paper. I was leisurely. Then I went out to do something I do now and then: I put out some milk in the back of my building where some stray cats often hang out. I waited, kept hoping the cats would come and find the milk; I haven't seen them do that yet. I had a dream last night. I was looking toward my window and three calico cats hopped onto my windowsill. I was so happy to see them there. Why would I have such a dream? Why was it so important? They were really beautiful, the colors on them. They changed a drab atmosphere into something spectacular and exciting. I had talked to Dad about that too when I visited, about feeding animals. He does it all the time. You know, when I was a kid I used to do that too—feed the animals, like Dad."

So once again the patient speaks of the same two points, one directly, one indirectly. Directly, she says that here is another way she is like her father, in a nice way, feeding animals, cooking food, and not only like him in his or her potential violence. And she says indirectly that something can "change a drab atmosphere into something spectacular and exciting." I believe *that* is what she was trying to report about her symptom; it changes her from the ordinary, the drab, to someone special.

This time the analyst responded to it. After the patient's remark that her father also fed animals and that she did it even in childhood, the analyst says: "There's another connection with him. You've given me a very different picture of him today." The patient concludes the session: "He's always done nice things. My aunts and uncles always said that he was the one they called on when they ran into difficulty. That was such a contrast to my experience of him."

I give the fourth session of the week more succinctly. The patient referred back to the previous day a couple of times, especially to having tuned out the analyst's voice at one point, now saying she didn't want the analyst to tell her what was going on; she was afraid she would have no choice, she said, but to accept the analyst's view of things, and she instead wanted more room to figure things out for herself. *Costumes* came in about a third of the way through the session by way of a dream. People were in costumes, among them herself and an old friend. In the dream, she said, "I reached out my hand and put it on his arm. I wanted this contact with him." Her thoughts soon went to loss, specifically to her experience of the loss of the analyst as each session came to an end. And then she went to what I mentioned at the outset—her reference to the session of the day before, of not listening to the analyst, wanting to figure things out for herself. Here she paused, and then her thoughts went back to the Monday dream, the first session reported here. "I was thinking about the dream the other day, the blood streaming down and I knew it was part of a costume—after all those costumes I had seen at Mardi Gras." She next spoke of anger buried inside her, not wanting to see it, but the blood somehow giving evidence of it. The analyst noted: "But in the dream, you weren't afraid of it." This stimulated the patient to report two other memories, both about scary-appearing images that were not in fact scary at all. One involved costumes at a children's theater production, a seemingly frightening figure that was not so at all. The other involved a painting which at first glance seemed scary, but she saw it as pleasant as she looked more closely. The analyst again commented that the patient can get scared of things, then not want to see them, because of feelings and images inside herself. She seemed both to be saying that the patient defends against knowing her anger in this manner (as she had done in previous sessions) and to be giving recognition to what seemed a new step in the session—the patient's discovery that things were not so scary after all.

My speculation, consistent with my comments about the prior session, is that the costume had an *additional* meaning to the seeing and denying of dangerous aggression. And that is that the patient had a way of "dressing up." The costume, like the calico cats, was enlivening. And, as in the first dream of this session (its manifest content, I recognize, but associations are in the material of the session and the week), she made *contact* in the costume, contact with her "old friend." Can it be that the fears of aggression, perhaps originally and probably centrally organized around her terror when her father screamed and thrashed in the night, had taken on additional meanings over time? The meanings I propose are: (1) contact with her father—that is, an object relationship (in her mind)—by being like him; by wearing the same "costume" as he does (the dangerous aggression), and (2) a more individualized sense of self, a livelier "costume," not like one the "normal" or "ordinary" people wear—that is, a unique identification, valued though conflictual and disturbing. I believe that this is the case and, largely on the strength of the patient's associations in the third of these four sessions, that it is the central content of these particular sessions. The patient was dealing with her link to her father and her sense of her self; the analyst was dealing primarily with the patient's defensive avoidance of her anger. Both are significant. The question is which do we address when. That is what I have tried to illustrate with each of the examples given in this chapter—the clinical reasoning underlying the direction of the particular interpretive choices we make at a given moment.

8 The Use of Developmental Perspectives in Adult Clinical Practice

My impression is that most analysts who work with both children and adults feel strongly that their work with children and, more broadly, a developmental point of view profoundly affect their clinical work with adults. In discussing this view with others, however, I sense that while the influence is generally implicit in the analyst's thinking, it is difficult to make explicit. The last creatures that would discover water would be fish, and developmental thinkers and child analysts seem to be the fish in this case—that is, swimming in an environment (developmental thinking) so taken for granted that it becomes easy not even to notice it. Or, to shift metaphors, it is like the Molière character who discovers that he has been speaking prose all his life. A developmental perspective is often so intrinsic to the analyst's ways of

Originally published in *Contemporary Psychoanalysis* (1992) 28: 261–276 and adapted and expanded for this book.

working that he or she is scarcely aware of the way it enters in. It is the prose of the clinical work, and so prosaic that it is hardly noticed.

In this chapter, I undertake the job of making the implicit explicit. I do what I can toward that end, though aware that there may be many parts of my watery surround that I am still not noticing and hence am unable to articulate.

It is not the case that a developmental perspective is seen as *the* necessary approach to adult practice, and it is certainly not a sufficient one. There are no "shoulds" about it—that one does best by working, or ought to work, in such and such a developmentally informed way. In saying this, I take it for granted that we all have some conception of development and are interested in the particular development of the individual with whom we are working at any moment, but I take a "developmental perspective" to refer to something well beyond these ordinary and expectable orientations. It has to do with who one is, how one thinks, and how one understands the nature of the pathology and of the therapeutic impact as one sits with the patient.

A developmental perspective is only one among many guiding perspectives that analysts use. For some, the guiding perspective is that everything is conflict and compromise formation, and this view carries us far in the comprehension of clinical material. For some, the view that the here-and-now of the transference is the site where everything of significance is represented will also carry analytic understanding very far. And for some, a view of the free-associative process as a dialogue with significant objects—internalized, reshaped, reexternalized, identified with, sought after, fled from, and more—will also be an immensely productive mental set that governs analytic listening. One need not select among these in opposing ways, and one may add others as well—attention to the patient's affect, to countertransference responses, to language style, pace, and idiosyncrasy—as guiding beacons, as perspectives that shape and inform analytic listening. A developmental perspective need not be more basic, first among equals, or holier than thou.

Having said that, I summarize what I am able to come up with regarding the contributions of a developmental perspective. I attempt to translate the implicit to the explicit under seven headings: (1) the contributions of different databases to the evolution of general theory; (2) a view of development as proceeding lifelong and as represented concretely in the issues of everyday life; (3) some specific spin-offs of this lifespan view of development as they affect the clinical process, notably the contrasting roles of the holding environment (Winnicott, 1963a) and of the patient's autonomous functioning; (4) a specific recognition factor regarding marker behaviors associated with early developmental issues or phenomena; (5) construction work as it applies to analytic process in the area of defective ego function or object relations; (6) the "developmental work" of psychoanalysis (Fonagy and Target, 1996)—that is, construction work with respect to essentially normal developmental processes; and (7) an understanding of development as it enhances the adaptation of the patient and the reality testing of the analyst about the analytic process.

I intend my discussion of these points, as I expand on them, to be predominantly at the level of the conception of and interventions within clinical work. While not a programmatic scheme regarding the "how to" of clinical work, these *are* potentials within the treatment process. For me, they have all grown directly out of, and then fed back into, my day-to-day work. As I discuss them I retain my belief that this way of working does not take precedence over all others (indeed, the various guiding perspectives listed a moment ago are all ones I use). But I hope at least to shed light on the developmental perspective and its utility, both for a general view of the analytic process and for lighting up some of its specific nooks and crannies.

The Database and Theory

The first point on my list is the contribution of differing databases to the evolution of general theory. In the experimentally "pure" situation of psychoanalysis, working only with the patient's free associations, Freud and his followers in the first decades of psychoanalysis found it both possible and productive to see virtually all of a human life in terms of the person's wishes and his or her defenses against or affects in relation to them. That is, the database (free association) let the analyst hear about the impact of others, but only the patient's thoughts were available firsthand—and one could come to see how the patient elicited, or repetitiously responded to, phenomena in ways that revealed his or her own wishes and, under them (by inference), the "instinctual drives." Such, at least for Freud, coming from his particular scientific weltanschauung, was the theoretical choice he made. These phenomena were thought to be especially visible in the transference, where, it was then understood, the analyst's contribution was practically nil and the patient created the specific analytic landscape. Thus the patient was, so to speak, the "cause" of his or her own life. Other theoretical choices could be made, of course. Sullivan (1953) chose interpersonal relations, but perhaps in part because of *his* database—that is, work with schizophrenics, in whom basic human connectedness was often faulty.

The turn to child analysis expanded the original psychoanalytic database. Although wishes and their source in sexual and aggressive drives could be inferred from both speech and play, object relations (in the form of the impact of parents, gradually internalized) could not be ignored. And the significance of a functioning ego—evident both in the major changes in adaptation as the child matured and in the defects in ego function often clearly evident in relation to affect modulation, impulse control, judgment, and the like—brought an ego theory compellingly into view. Adult clinical psychoanalysis already required an ego theory to explain how learning and change were possible in development (and in analysis) and to account for intrapsychic defense; but child analysis gave this a big push forward.

Beyond child analysis, infant observation forced further modifications in basic theory. For there, the analytic observer had virtually no access to fantasy (and with it wish and inferred drive). But the database provided ample evidence of the importance of early object relations and of impressive developments in ego function. And within the arena of infant observation, the three major psychoanalytic baby-watchers—Spitz (1959), Winnicott (1965), and Mahler (Mahler, Pine, and Bergman, 1975)—each found it indispensable to theorize in terms of the gradual crystallization of a self, a self-other boundary, and a self-other tie.

So, as we would expect, the observational database affects theory, and a base of observation in child analysis and baby-watching makes rootedness in a "four psychologies" view both compelling and convincing. This view finds a core place developmentally for concepts centering on drive, ego, object relations, and self. It can naturally extend into adult clinical work, affecting how we formulate interpretations—that is, what content we think matters. I find that I speak comfortably to patients in the languages of drive, ego, object relations, and self, confident that these languages are not first derived from theory and then imposed on clinical data but, rather, come as close as possible to matching patients' recognizable inner experiences. Though it goes without saying that one can arrive at expansions in theory from many routes, the developmental route forces such expansions on the analytic observer with particular vividness.

Lifelong Development

A second impact of a developmental point of view in adult clinical work involves a view of development as taking place lifelong. This position has significant implications for our understandings of potentialities in the clinical process as well. The core idea is that life-as-lived is a developmental process continually presenting each of us with age-related adaptive tasks; these new tasks are often approached by bringing to bear old styles of defending and mastering and, along with these, old wishes, repetitions, failures, and enactments. Figuratively, the new task is grabbed by old solutions; thus the past is lived out in the present, similar to the way it is lived out in the transference—the "adaptive task" confronting the patient as a result of entry into analysis.

The day-to-day experience of living requires each of us to confront developmental issues active at a particular time. For those of us in the field of psychoanalysis, for example, these issues may have to do with learning to be a psychoanalyst, or becoming a teacher or administrator in an aspect of the field, or coming to terms with what we have or have not achieved, or facing retirement or age-related losses of function. On the personal side of things, we may be dealing with mate-finding, or the end of a significant relationship, or becoming a parent or a grandparent, or aging, illness, loss of friends, and death. The developmental tasks are never-ending. We can never feel for more than a moment, Here I am, now I can stand still.

Our theorists have not explicated this situation much, except for Erikson (1950), who did so only schematically. But it is true nonetheless that we are always contending with the developmental issues of our particular age. We each know what daily life-as-lived feels like. It is not only in childhood and adolescence that we can see life in terms of developmental tasks—for example, differentiating self and other, cementing core relationships to caretakers, achieving bodily self-care, entering school, learning the world of childhood games, chants, rituals (Stone and Church, 1973), coping with the bodily changes of adolescence and the renewed push for separation from the home of childhood. Not only in childhood but throughout life development continually foists new tasks on us—marriage, parenting, occupational success and failure, aging, to name a few of the most obvious ones.

What we readily recognize to be true for ourselves is also true for our patients, child or adult. Inside the sessions they live lives organized around transference, fantasy, repetition, memory, and current interaction. But in the world outside, they live around the developmental issues I have already listed. When recognized for what they are, these issues should and ordinarily do have a significant place in the analysis as well.

I am not arguing for a psychoanalysis of current events—of the *there*-and-now of the extratransference world. But I do argue for recognition of the potential that particular extratransference events have in elucidating the patient's style of mastering or defending against new stimuli, or of his or her living out fantasies in subtle ways, and the past on which these are based. We work with transference because it is where the heat, the immediacy of affect, is most likely to be; thus it makes insight and conviction possible when something is understood. When something else is the "hot" area, however—for example, the death of a significant person, or a major job failure—we follow the material there. Developmental tasks, too, can be hot areas if recognized as such. The developmental process continually presents us with new, age-related, adaptive demands; we often see in treatment how the person brings old, faulted fantasies and character styles to bear on the resolution of these demands. Old ways often overtake our new opportunities and imbue them with a familiar sameness. And the patient's affect is caught up in the new mate, the new child, the new career stage, the new aspect of bodily functioning. As such, these new developmental issues, just like the transference, become battle-grounds where the past is played out in the present, potentially with great profit for the analytic work when understood.

Safety and Autonomy

The structure of the analytic process itself can usefully be seen as a mirror of the basic structure of the developmental process. (I have discussed this point briefly earlier, but I want to enlarge on it here.) I refer to those features within the analytic process that are captured by Winnicott's (1963a) concept of the holding environment, on the one hand, and those having to do with the patient's essential aloneness, independence, or responsibility for autonomous functioning, on the other. The analytic process, like good parenting, inherently includes both the context of safety and the expectation of autonomous functioning and weaves the two together.

I think it fair to say that analysts as a group believe that the infant and young child thrive best in the atmosphere of safety the mother provides—the view that Winnicott intended to capture with his concept of the holding environment. It includes such things as meeting the infant's needs, modulating stimulation so that it does not become overwhelming, and altogether responding reliably to the infant. But were we able to wrap the infant in such an environment, to meet its every need, surely we would stunt the development of those active and autonomous features that make a person a full human being. For-tunately, the child's biologically programmed thrust forward (say, into bodily self-control, crawling, walking) and the caretaker's inevitable failure to meet every need ensure that the child will not stay wrapped in a holding environment that becomes a prison.

An analysis, too, is built around the features of safety and autonomy; and I believe that together the two make constructive change possible. That is, these two features, which foster the earliest developments of the person, in fact foster development lifelong. Surely one of Freud's greatest contributions was his creation of the analytic situation—two persons who come together with frequency and regularity, with one freely associating and the other listening with evenly suspended attention. Like the invention of the telescope or the microscope, the creation of this new method of observation created a myriad of new learnings. But while we generally think of Freud's creation in terms of the opportunity for listening to free associations and observing the evolution of the transference, we should not fail to note that the created analytic situation is built around that same holding environment, on the one hand, and the patient's responsibility for autonomous functioning, on the other. These are part of the background of the analytic situation; they are the stage on which the action happens and which enables it to happen. The "holding" aspect refers to the analyst's regularity and reliability, to his or her direction of attention to the patient, to the patient as the whole agenda, the center of concern. That holding environment can provide a safe place where inner exploration, and change, and loving can be tried out, but also hating, seduction, rebellion, and autonomous activity itself. But no patient experiences an analysis simply as a safe—a "held"—place. Quite the reverse. We ask the patient, and the patient learns, to work hard, to venture into threatening inner places, and to carry a significant responsibility for the process. These two together, the provision of safety and the requirement of autonomy, are developmentally forwarding. The work on the "content" (of associations, transference, memory, fantasy) progresses because of this developmentally geared framework of holding and individual responsibility, activity, and autonomy.

In addition, I find that this understanding of the basic framework affects my thinking during the process and sometimes my interventions, or noninterventions, as well. Let me take first the atmosphere of "holding." Supervising (as I did formerly) in a municipal hospital psychiatric clinic, I have long had ongoing contact with severely disorganized and traumatized patients who seem far from ideally suited to insight-oriented therapeutic work. But insight—that is, the use of our distinctively human cognitive capacities—is a great tool for adaptation, and my effort over the years (I now see with hindsight) was to find ways to make it available to these seemingly "unsuited" patients. I developed a way of working that I captured in an epigrammatic formulation: interpret in the context of support rather than, as in analysis, in the context of abstinence (Pine, 1984). I found that this particular way of working, the end result of numerous trial-and-error efforts to bring the potentialities of dynamically oriented insight therapy to our patients, went well and far. But having done this with my often quite disorganized and not highly verbal supervised patients, I began to think about it also in terms of more traditional psychoanalysis. I now believe that some such concept as the seemingly self-contradictory term *supportive psychoanalysis* should be part of our vocabulary, or perhaps even better, *psychoanalysis with support*. I prefer this to the term *parameters* (Eissler, 1953) because it is more descriptive, more explicit, more provocative perhaps, and thus potentially encourages productive thought. In recent decades, many analysts—for reasons of humanitarianism, economics, and the wish to practice their profession—have worked with some patients in analysis who, years before, they might have considered to be unsuited to its rigors, perhaps because of the extent of anxiety or impulsivity or general life chaos. Small, self-conscious increases in the holding environment often make an analysis possible—an analysis that feels exactly like one that does not have these modifications. I am referring to such discrete (and very occasional) interventions as, for example, saying to a patient who is disorganized (in too prolonged a silence): "I'm here and listening; I'll speak when I have something to say." Or even simply, "Do you need me to speak now?" Or as another example, with a patient who fears (with some justice) being overwhelmed by his or her spontaneous thoughts: "You can say them when you feel ready; we have plenty of time"; this statement often makes relatively immediate expression tolerable to the patient, as the inner sense of pressure is diminished. An awareness of the developmentally forwarding aspect of the built-in holding environment of analysis thus also permits its more active enhancement when clinically appropriate.

The active "use" that I make of the other built-in aspect of the analytic situation—that is, the autonomous activity required of the patient—is of a very different order. I discuss it around my conception of what is happening even when "nothing" is happening in the analysis. By "nothing" in this context I mean "no insight."

I find that, when I sit with a patient who is feeling something deeply and perhaps painfully, but without immediately understanding what is going on, I nonetheless have the inner sense that something valuable *is* going on—that is, that to bear intense affect in the safe presence of another is an exercise of ego capacity that is developmentally forwarding. Similarly, as Loewald (1960) points out, when the patient struggles to put inner events into words so as to reach the analyst's understanding, something developmentally forwarding is again happening—in the act of putting inner events into words, perhaps for the first time—even if nothing further is clearly understood. Similarly, when the patient experiences the relationship to the analyst as troubled—as, say, a failure in empathy—or when the patient feels enraged for some other reason, the constant rediscovery that a relationship can—in Winnicott's (1963b) term—"survive" is also developmentally forwarding.

Does such a view give us false comfort? Does it justify a failure of empathy or insight or capacity to interpret tactfully? I think not. Insight is indispensable in the analytic process. It is hardly true, however, that we always understand or that the patient-analyst relationship is always untroubled. But the autonomous exercise of the patient's capacities for affect experience and verbalization and for sustaining delay in the face of not as yet understood or mastered phenomena, as well as for coming to tolerate and work through disruptions in the analytic relationship, is as significant a part of the analytic process as of development itself.

I call these events "developmentally forwarding" as an automatic reflection of working within a developmental perspective. Just as the holding environment the mother provides permits the infant and young child to move forward with developmental tasks, so the inevitable and developmentally required maternal failure to meet every need makes it possible for the growing child to begin to assume self-regulating and inner-processing functions for itself. Theorists as different as Winnicott (1963c), Mahler (Mahler et al., 1975), and Kohut (1971) have all pointed to the need for and value of this maternal "failure," provided that it comes in small doses. So, too, as we sit, "failing," behind the analytic couch; so, too, for the patient in the analytic process. We do not have to plan to fail the patient in this developmentally forwarding way; we inevitably will, often (though not always) to the patient's eventual benefit.

Developmental Markers

A fourth feature of the developmental perspective that one can bring to adult analytic work has to do with the recognition of marker phenomena, markers of early developmental issues. These serve as familiar landmarks that, at times, tell us which general territory we are in. Thus, to take a familiar marker from a time late in early development, if a patient is regularly describing rivalrous triangular relationships, we are alerted to issues of the oedipal phase.

Let me, by way of illustration, mention one of what I consider to be Mahler's (Mahler et al., 1975) important contributions. Many before her had written of the presumed emergence of the very young child from a state of blurred self-other boundaries. But by studying this firsthand in the infant and toddler, Mahler was able to describe behaviors and affects characteristic of various stages of the process through which that development takes place—for example, elated mood, incessant activity, low-keyedness, and refueling in the practicing subphase of the separation-individuation process, or sad mood, coercion, and shadowing in the rapprochement subphase. Seeing such behaviors—or adult forms of them—later, during clinical work, may alert us to the possibility that the issues of that particular phase are now active in the analysis. That is, familiarity with early development and the developmental literature can expand our capacity for awareness of such phenomena when their markers, their residue, occur before our very eyes and ears.

Here are two recent examples from my own clinical work, having to do with other early developmental domains. A woman in her fifties, the mother of two grown children, was recalling how important it had been for her, when her children were very young, to be sensitively in tune with their needs. By contrast, she said, her own parents' responses had always seemed "at a tangent" to hers, going off in another direction somehow, and leaving her with a peculiarly unsettled and unreal feeling about her communications to them or her actions. She spoke of how she would then make an effort to "adjust" what she said to their response, but she recalled a sickened, almost nauseous, feeling that would accompany these "adjusting" efforts. Suddenly what sprung into my mind was Winnicott's (1960) formulation regarding the significance of the infant's "spontaneous gesture," met or unmet by the parent. He suggests that when the infant emits something expressive—say, an outstretched hand or a cry or a smile—and the caretaker's response is in tune with it, the infant not only experiences a sense of "fit" or a satisfaction or confirmation but learns, presumably by conditioning, that it is safe and pleasurable to emit such spontaneous gestures. By contrast, when these gestures are missed or inappropriately matched by the caretaker, not only is there an immediate experience of nonsatisfaction, disconfirmation, and letdown, but the emitting of such responses becomes conditioned out—that is, negatively reinforced. Winnicott links this outcome to the beginning of false-self development: the young child begins to produce initiatives that will suit the surround (and elicit a response) whether or not the initiatives comfortably and naturally flow from the child's state in itself.

My point is that my familiarity with this idea in the developmental literature and its reality and vividness to me in relation to my knowledge of childhood permitted me to recognize in my patient's report about her family something that gave me, and then us, a whole new perspective on aspects of her pathology that until that time had been sensed but not subjected to clear description or understanding. My patient's "adjustments" to the parental response, accompanied by the inner disorientation signaled by the nausea, reflected this loss of self-feeling, a "false-self" position in Winnicott's terms.

Here is a second instance of the value of marker behaviors as cues, also drawn from my own clinical work. (I have already referred to this case in Chapter 6.) The patient, in analysis and working well in it, showed certain delimited defects in impulse control which we came to understand as stemming from early identifications and experiences of seduction. She felt a real danger of acting on her sexual impulses toward me. Much sexual fantasy had been expressed and analyzed for its meaning, but with no impact on the specific sense of imminent loss of control. At one point in the analysis I sensed that a spontaneous change was taking place in the sessions. The patient was again bringing in detailed sexual fantasies involving me. But I found that I was hearing them in a new light. She seemed less threatened by them now, less anxious, willing to risk arousal without, apparently, feeling in danger of becoming overwhelmed. I suddenly thought of her as being engaged in a form of play—play with fantasy, play with the limits of her capacity, play with a simultaneous sense of risk and of safety in my presence. In retrospect I can see that I was aware that this was just what the young child does with play, and that there was no reason to think that this ends with childhood. At this point, for a period of the analysis I did not interpret any of the fantasy content but only pointed out the patient's different use of it and my sense that it did not seem so dangerous now. I am quite convinced that this was one of the steps that ultimately led to secure impulse control in this area. In addition, my recognition of the mental and affective quality of play in this patient's then-current productions stemmed from my knowledge of childhood and of the use of play for mastery and from my developmental perspective.

I give both of these examples—of the failure of response to the spontaneous gesture and of the emergence and use of a playlike process—to illustrate that familiarity with the child in the immediacy of its experience and familiarity with the child analytic literature may increase our recognition of marker behaviors that help us find our bearings in additional ways within the patient's clinical productions.

Ego "Construction"

A fifth area where a developmental perspective can productively enter adult clinical work is in a particular kind of psychological construction work. As indicated in my brief comments on the patient just described, the presence of a circumscribed ego defect does not render an analysis unworkable. Similarly, as I mentioned when I spoke of the holding environment, the use at times of carefully calibrated supportive interventions can make analysis possible for some patients who otherwise seem unanalyzable, because of their potential to be overwhelmed or their fragility. Overall, a developmental perspective can enhance certain kinds of construction work in an analysis—that is, the construction of control or defense or where necessary in other areas of defective ego functioning. Developmental knowledge gives us some basis for beginning to think about how object constancy, the signal function of anxiety, or adequate control over impulse might have failed to develop earlier, and how we might facilitate such developments now in the adult. Our knowledge here is far from complete, but we are not fully in the dark. By asking such questions we not only draw on developmental understanding but also make so-called supportive work interesting intellectually and remove it from the intellectual wasteland in which it has been allowed to languish (Pine, 1976; but see, more recently, Werman, 1984; Rockland, 1989; and Wallerstein, 1985). As an illustration I again refer to Fleming's (1975) paper on failed object constancy and my own just mentioned case of circumscribed defect in impulse control as examples of such work. In each of these cases, the work involved not the mechanical application of some developmental principle (I do not know what such a principle would be) but rather recognizing and utilizing spontaneously emerging aspects of the patient's productions that had developmentally linked potential.

In my discussion of expansions in theory, I suggested that the database of child analysis and infant and child observation forces a receptivity to such expansions—that is, to the inclusion in one's theory of mind of drive, ego, object relational, and self issues. I believe that the child development database similarly promotes a receptivity to concepts such as ego defect or object relational deficit (as discussed in Chapter 6).

Developmental Work

The "developmental work" of analysis is another application of a developmental perspective in adult clinical work. Fonagy and Target (1996) use this term to refer to significant parts of the analytic work with children, as carried out at Hampstead under Anna Freud's direction, when developmental disorders were understood to exist side by side with conflict disorders. This, too, is a form of "construction work," as I am using the term, but now the construction work of the normal developmental process, which does not stop happening in adulthood in general or in analysis in particular. I have referred to such developmental phenomena at various places in this book because they are intrinsic to a developmental orientation and inherent in analytic work as seen from a developmental perspective. Let me list several of them:

(1) The naming of affects (Katan, 1961) is an activity of the analyst that compares to a parallel activity of a parent and can serve in the differentiation of affects, in bringing them from the inchoate to the communicable, from the thoroughly private to the shared.

(2) The analytic process enables the patient to find words for inner experiences in the act of attempting to communicate them to the analyst (Loewald, 1960); in so doing, and when these experiences have never before been put into words, the patient (again) moves these experiences from the inchoate to the named, from the private to the

shared; these acts of clarification can be productive in themselves even apart from whatever interpretive understandings may later be reached with respect to them.

(3) Included in this developmental work is the analyst's confirmation of the patient's reality—not only by explicit statement but also, more silently, by incorporating what the patient has said into the analyst's communications, letting them thereby exist as phenomena in the world out there, not only in the patient's subjective world; for the patient this often gives a measure of confirmation and objectivity to particular communications, especially those that he or she views as not fully fact-based but as partially formulative or subjective.

(4) The analyst's continuing to attend to and work with the patient, matter-of-factly and appreciatively (Schafer, 1983), even in the face of what the patient may experience as reprehensible or shameful confessions, automatically imparts to the patient a measure of respect and esteem through the analyst's maintenance of a basic working attitude, without the need for any special reassurance.

(5) The patient's and the analyst's "survival" (Winnicott, 1963b) in the face of aggressive or seductive confrontations in the analytic space imparts to the patient a belief that aggression need not destroy, that seduction need not seduce, that a steady relationship can continue despite such assaults and threats; this progressively enables the patient to own powerful urges, seen as less dangerous, as simply part of the self.

And (6) the analyst's continuing work orientation imparts to the patient the possibility of hope, of belief in a future, of transformation and change.

Each of these is potentially embodied in the unique relationship of the analytic process and communicated to the patient through the ordinary working stance of the analyst. They are parts of the new object relationship. None of them necessarily occurs automatically, however. As I discussed in Chapter 3 regarding the so-called nonspecific effects of an analysis, there are likely to be dynamic interferences with the patient's capacity to experience some or many of these potentially development-enhancing effects in benign form. Nonetheless these are directions in which an analysis moves over time, and as one or another of the dynamic interferences are identified, analyzed, and altered, the developmentally forwarding experiences that are inherent in and inseparable from the new object relationship with the analyst can become useful to the patient. All this is outside of interpretation, though considerable interpretation may be required before the patient can experience something of value in the relationship itself. And all these forms of impact in analysis mirror forms of developmental impact of the good-enough parent on the child.

Developmental Understanding in Itself

The value of developmental understanding in enhancing the adaptation of both the patient and the therapist is a view that derives from a developmental perspective. Quite a few years ago, when Merton Gill was just beginning to develop his ideas on working within the here-and-now of the transference, I asked him after a lecture whether he didn't think that the patient's attainment of an understanding of his or her life story in its fullness was not also (in addition to work in the transference) a route to a better clinical outcome. He said something like: "No, that's important to *you*, Fred, because you're a developmental psychologist; but patients care only about getting rid of their symptoms and anxieties."[1]

But I do not think this is important only to me; or perhaps it is important to me and I convey this, subtly or not so subtly, to my patients. It seems that patients, my patients at least, get a great deal from the fullest possible understanding of their life story: a sense of ownership of a whole life and an understanding of where they came from and why they are as they are; some acceptance of limitations that were not overcome, or of years experienced as lost years, or of the

1. Now, Gill (1990) says, he "would not be as extreme as I was then, but am still of the opinion that different analysts, based on their own intellectual predilections, place emphasis more on the one than the other, perhaps in response to what they subtly sense to be more important to the particular patient—in other words, both a less extreme and a more interactive view."

reality of failed parents or of parent capacities that the patient, because of inner conflict, could not make use of; or the discovery of loving feelings toward a parent where it was believed there was only hate or noncontact—all of which permits one to move on with life, like Coleridge's Ancient Mariner, a sadder but wiser person; and a framework that is valuable in subsequent self-analysis, enlarging the context for understanding. I believe that the achievement by the patient of a developmental perspective on his or her own life is invaluable, potentially in all of these ways.

And for the therapist or analyst? Apart from the fact that the therapist is or was also a patient, and that what I just said I believe to be true of all of us as well, there is an additional gain. A developmental perspective can give us a respect for the limitations of our work and a sense of modesty about our achievements. This works on both sides of the ledger. For if we come to know the repetitiveness of developmental experiences, the power of trauma, the rigidity of reliance on achieved adaptations, pathological or not, then we can be more forgiving of ourselves and of the analytic process itself for doing just so much and not more for this or that particular patient. Furthermore, if we are aware of the immense adaptive and transforming potentials that most human beings are capable of and that, for many, inhere in the developmental process itself, potentials that are demonstrated in at least some areas in their growing up, we may be more modest in our beliefs about what we have accomplished, aside from re-freeing the developmental process. Freud (1919) pointed out that we can content ourselves with analysis; the work of synthesis is work that patients will do, often automatically, on their own. Neither of these points is meant to say that we cannot or do not do a great deal in the treatment. I believe that we can and do; but recognition and understanding of limits never hurt.

Concluding Remarks

I have sketched out a number of developmental perspectives that I believe can enhance divergent aspects of adult clinical work. They range widely and include the following:

Expansions in theory are made more convincing and sometimes clearer when we find certain phenomena in the child as well as in the adult. Phenomena of ego development, object relations, and self formation, in addition to the phenomena of the psychosexual phases, are particularly vivid in the developing child and are therefore compelling in their theoretical consequences. The different observational database thus makes for a receptivity toward thinking conceptually in multiple-model terms.

Life-as-lived is a developmental process, and development itself forces new adaptive tasks on the individual at each age, in adulthood as in childhood. Often old forms of solution are brought to bear on these new adaptive tasks, and the past comes alive in the patient's efforts to deal with them. Like work in the transference, where the past is also in the present, affectively meaningful work, work with immediacy, can be done as these new developmental tasks are commandeered by old modes of solution and the patient suffers them in the process of attempting to deal with them.

The holding environment fosters development, is built into the analytic setup, and can sometimes be specifically enhanced with valuable therapeutic effect—often facilitating, not impeding, the continuance of an analytic process. Similarly, autonomous functioning is necessary for development and is built into the analytic setup; recognizing it can help us to understand much that is going on when the patient is simply working at his or her analytic task, not necessarily achieving any insight. Together these two features embody the recognition of an analysis as itself having core features of a developmentally facilitating process: safety and demand, holding and autonomy.

Certain phenomena may be residual markers of old, unsettled phase-specific conflicts or developmental failures; their recognition may help the therapist form hypotheses that may enhance understanding. The child analytic literature, the child development literature, and infant and child observations can be sources of hypotheses regarding both these marker behaviors and the opportunities for corrective action around ego defects.

Knowledge of how certain ego functions ordinarily develop or fail to develop may, within a usual analytic process, provide a background for recognizing developmental opportunities in regions of ego defect (for example, inadequate object constancy or impulse control, the failure to move from traumatic to signal anxiety). While our general knowledge regarding ways to overcome developmental failures is minimal, we sometimes *can* recognize routes taken toward that end that are spontaneously created by individual patients within their analyses—and, recognizing them, we can work with them productively.

A great deal of "developmental work" is carried by the new object relationship to the analyst in the unique process of analysis. This can be developmentally facilitating for the adult patient as it is for the child with the parent. While it requires no special work from the analyst to create the developmental opportunity, patients will often have dynamic interferences that will prevent them from experiencing these relational features usefully, and these interferences can gradually come into interpretive focus.

Having a fully rounded view of their life story may enhance patients' adaptation, self-acceptance, sense of being sadder but wiser, and later self-analyses. Analysts, too, gain from understanding their own and their patient's development as well as the developmental process itself; this provides a grounding for coping with the heat of the analytic encounter and a basis for reality testing regarding both the obstacles to and the possibilities for change.

In scanning the contributions of a developmental perspective in psychoanalytic work, I do not intend to create any clinical injunctions regarding that work. These ideas, like all of our theories, are best held in the back of the working analyst's mind, not in the forefront. My view is that it is sometimes development, sometimes the transference, sometimes affect, sometimes language usage, sometimes behavior in the session, and sometimes dreams that orient one's understandings and interventions. Multiple models of clinical listening as well as of theoretical conceptualization will serve us best.

Postscript

Early in this book I referred to Berman's (1991) remark that psycho-analysis has multitudes of mini-theories of how mind works but just does not know how to put them all together. We also, I would now add, have multitudes of mini-theories of technique, and in this case I believe we are best off not devoting much effort to putting them all together. Each of us needs some guidelines, and free association, evenly suspended attention, neutrality, abstinence, and relative anonymity remain the salient ones for me. But I now see these as baselines to which I generally return rather than as positions from which I never stray. To put it in another way, I see them as positions from which I start to work until I learn better what a particular analysis seems to entail and require. Technique is in the details. Holding a too-powerful theory of technique can make trouble for the patient.

I certainly do not have an "anything goes" attitude about technique, and I assume that the reader by now is aware of my own blend of essential conservatism and (I hope) an openness to exploration and discovery. I have tried to convey that in my selection of topics, which range from the vital and continuing applicability of ego psychology in psychoanalytic work to questions of self-disclosure; from conflict-oriented interpretive work to attempts to enter the difficult area of technique with the developmental pathologies (defects in ego function and deficits in the environmental provision); from a heavy emphasis on the achievement of insight to a recognition of the core role of relational effects even at the moment of interpretation; and from an attempt to describe clinical and technical phenomena in a search for consensus to a recognition (nonetheless) of the highly individualized nature of the analytic process, a mix of the character and education of the analyst with the history and personality of the patient.

There is a way, as I see it, to position oneself productively within the current diverse array of possibilities regarding clinical technique, and that is to view them as reflections of *patient characteristics.* The array of possibilities does of course reflect and emanate from different theories of mind and from individual differences among analysts in style, character, training, and personal history. But I now consider that they also reflect the clinical possibilities and *requirements* created by the character, history, and style of individual patients.

Along these lines, I earlier (Pine, 1990) developed the position that issues of drive, ego, object relations, and self have found their way into our theories because they are centrally organizing themes in one or another of our *patients,* each more in one than another, more at one time in the analysis than at another, more central overall for one patient than for another—though each theme is relevant to some extent for all patients. Or, from a quite different starting point but still culminating in a view of the characteristics of the patient, I have suggested that "empathic failure" is best seen not as a concept about clumsiness or failed attunement in *analysts* but as about patients. That is, some patients react to failed attunement with major disorganization, withdrawal, pain, or rage while others go right past it; this tells us something about the *patient* and may at times force particular ways of working clinically.

So, too, I contend, for the array of technical possibilities discussed in this book. Despite the major contributions of the analyst's style or theory, some patients—because of who they are and how they create the analytic situation (if they are given the space to do so)—will force (for example) a more intersubjective, two-person way of working and some a more intrapsychic, one-person way. Some will create a powerful demand for, or an urge in the analyst toward, self-disclosure (whether or not the analyst acts on this), and some will not (though they may *wish* to know about the analyst). Some will draw more from object usage—the analyst as auxiliary ego, self-object, provider of corrective experience—and some more from interpretation and self-found clarification of the inner life. Some will bring ego defects, developmental pathologies, or object relational deficits into the work as central features of their character and pathology, and others will bring these in only peripherally. And so on. Clinical technique, too, like theory, is additive, not substitutive. As we have learned more about patients, we have created more theories—of mind, of development, of pathology, and of technique.

With this mix, and in the absence of a general theory of technique or even a generally agreed-on theory of mind, is there any sense in which psychoanalysis can claim to be a science? I believe there is, but it is limited. We know a great deal about mental functioning, about how character and personality are formed, about how mind works in the current moment, and about how to have an effect on a person's mental function. Therein lies any claim to science we can make. It is a strong claim in spite of its limitations. When it comes to the specifics of technique on a moment-to-moment basis, however, that claim cannot be made with anything near equal force. In that situation we are highly dependent on individual talent, and the entire process is a creative endeavor in essential ways. But creativity of the best sort stems from knowledge, and I do not believe we should neglect how much we *do* know.

I have tried here to give some thoughts based on my clinical experiences in the hope that they will produce more thoughts in other analysts. The more possibilities we can have in mind, the better off we are in the situation of analytic listening.

References

Abend, S. M. (1990). The psychoanalytic process: Motives and obstacles in the search for clarification. *Psychoanal. Q.* 59: 532–549.

Abraham, K. (1921). Contributions to the theory of the anal character. In *Selected Papers.* New York: Basic Books, 1953, 370–392.

—— (1924). The influence of anal eroticism on character formation. In *Selected Papers.* New York: Basic Books, 1953, 393–406.

Abrams, S. (1990). The psychoanalytic process: The developmental and the integrative. *Psychoanal. Q.* 59: 650–677.

Alexander, F. (1948). *Fundamentals of Psychoanalysis.* New York: Norton.

—— (1956). *Psychoanalysis and Psychotherapy.* New York: Norton.

Anthony, E. J. (1970). The reaction of parents to adolescents and to their behavior. In *Parenthood: Its Psychology and Psychopathology,* ed. E. J. Anthony and T. Benedek. Boston: Little, Brown, 307–324.

Arlow, J. (1969a). Unconscious fantasy and disturbances of conscious experience. *Psychoanal. Q.* 38: 1–27.

—— (1969b). Fantasy, memory, and reality testing. *Psychoanal. Q.* 38: 28–51.

—— (1984). The psychoanalytic process in regard to the development of transference and interpretation. In *Psychoanalysis: The Vital Issues. Vol. 2: Clinical Psychoanalysis and Its Applications,* ed. G. H. Pollock and J. E. Gedo. New York: Int. Univ. Press, 21–44.

Arlow, J., and Brenner, C. (1990). The psychoanalytic process. *Psychoanal. Q.* 59: 678–692.

Aron, L. (1990). Free association and changing models of mind. *J. Amer. Acad. Psychoanal.* 18: 439–459.

Bach, S. (1994). *The Language of Perversion and the Language of Love.* Northvale, N.J.: Aronson.

Balint, M. (1968). *The Basic Fault.* London: Tavistock.

Berman, G. (1991). Discussion of "Drive, Ego, Object, and Self." Toronto Psychoanalytic Society, Toronto, Canada.

Boesky, D. (1990). The psychoanalytic process and its components. *Psychoanal. Q.* 59: 550–584.

Bollas, C. (1983). Expressive uses of the countertransference. *Contemp. Psychoanal.* 19: 1–34.

—— (1987). *The Shadow of the Object.* New York: Columbia Univ. Press.

Brenner, C. (1976). *Psychoanalytic Technique and Psychic Conflict.* New York: Int. Univ. Press

Broucek, F. J. (1991). *Shame and the Self.* New York: Guilford.

Busch, F. (1995). *The Ego at the Center of Clinical Technique.* Northvale, N.J.: Aronson.

Coen, S. J. (1986). The sense of defect. *J. Amer. Psychoanal. Assn.* 34: 47–67.

Compton, A. (1990). Psychoanalytic process. *Psychoanal. Q.* 59: 585–598.

Cooper, A. (1987). Changes in psychoanalytic ideas: Transference interpretation. *J. Amer. Psychoanal. Assn.* 35: 77–98.

Couch, A. (1995). Anna Freud's adult analytic technique: Classical analysis. *Int. J. Psychoanal.* 76: 153–172.

deJonghe, F., Rijnierse, P., and Janssen, R. (1992). The role of support in psychoanalysis. *J. Amer. Psychoanal. Assn.* 40: 475–490.

Deutsch, H. (1930). Hysterical fate neurosis. In *Neurosis and Character Types.* New York: Int. Univ. Press, 1965, 14–28.

—— (1942). Some forms of emotional disturbance and their relation to schizophrenia. *Psychoanal. Q.* 11: 301–331.

Dewald, P. A. (1990). Conceptualizations of the psychoanalytic process. *Psychoanal. Q.* 59: 693–711.

Eissler, K. (1953). The effect of the structure of the ego on psychoanalytic technique. *J. Amer. Psychoanal. Assn.* 1: 104–143.

Erikson, E. H. (1950). *Childhood and Society.* New York: Norton.

Ferenczi, S. (1933). On the confusion of tongues between adults and the child. In

Final Contributions to the Problems and Methods of Psychoanalysis. New York: Basic Books, 1955, 155–167.

Fleming, J. (1975). Some observations on object constancy in the psychoanalysis of adults. *J. Amer. Psychoanal. Assn.* 23: 743–754.

Fonagy, P., and Moran, G. S. (1991). Understanding psychic change in child psychoanalysis. *Int. J. Psychoanal.* 72: 15–22.

Fonagy, P., and Target, M. (1996). Outcome predictors in child psychoanalysis. *J. Amer. Psychoanal. Assn.* 44: 27–77.

Freud, A. (1936). The ego and the mechanisms of defense. In *The Writings of Anna Freud. Vol. 2.* New York: Int. Univ. Press, 1966, 1–191.

—— (1974). A psychoanalytic view of developmental psychopathology. In *The Writings of Anna Freud. Vol. 8.* New York: Int. Univ. Press, 1981, 57–74.

Freud, S. (1894). The neuro-psychoses of defense. *S.E.,* 3: 45–61.

—— (1900). The interpretation of dreams. *S.E.,* 4 and 5: 1–621.

—— (1905). Three essays on the theory of sexuality. *S.E.,* 7: 135–243.

—— (1908). Character and anal eroticism. *S.E.,* 9: 169–175.

—— (1912). Recommendations to physicians practicing psychoanalysis. *S.E.,* 12: 111–120.

—— (1916–17). Introductory lectures on psychoanalysis: Lecture 25, Anxiety. *S.E.,* 16: 392–411.

—— (1919). Lines of advance in psychoanalytic therapy. *S.E.,* 17: 159–168.

—— (1920). Beyond the pleasure principle. *S.E.,* 18: 7–64.

—— (1923). The ego and the id. *S.E.,* 19: 12–66.

—— (1926). Inhibitions, symptoms, and anxiety. *S.E.,* 20: 87–172.

—— (1930). Civilization and its discontents. *S.E.,* 21: 64–145.

—— (1933). New introductory lectures on psychoanalysis. *S.E.,* 22: 5–182.

—— (1937). Analysis terminable and interminable. *S.E.,* 23: 216–253.

Gedo, J. E. (1994). Academicism, romanticism, and science in the psychoanalytic enterprise. *Psychoanal. Inquiry* 14: 295–312.

Gill, M. M. (1979). The analysis of the transference. *J. Amer. Psychoanal. Assn. Supp.* 27: 263–288.

—— (1982). *Analysis of Transference. Vol. 1: Theory and Technique.* New York: Int. Univ. Press.

—— (1983). The interpersonal paradigm and the degree of the analyst's involvement. *Contemp. Psychoanal.* 19: 200–237.

—— (1984). Psychoanalysis and psychotherapy: A revision. *Int. Rev. Psychoanal.* 11: 161–179.

—— (1990). Personal communication.

—— (1994). *Psychoanalysis in Transition.* Hillsdale, N.J.: Analytic Press.

Goldberg, A. (1978). *The Psychology of the Self: A Casebook.* New York: Int. Univ. Press.

Gray, P. (1994). *The Ego and Analysis of Defense.* Northvale, N.J.: Aronson.

Green, A. (1993). Discussion at meetings of the International Psychoanalytic Association, Amsterdam.

Grossman, L. (1996). The analyst's influence. *Psychoanal. Q.* 65: 681–692.

Hanly, C. (1990). The concept of truth in psychoanalysis. *Int. J. Psychoanal.* 71: 375–383.

Hartmann, H. (1939). *Ego Psychology and the Problem of Adaptation.* New York: Int. Univ. Press, 1958.

—— (1950). Comments on the psychoanalytic theory of the ego. *Psychoanal. Study Child* 5: 74–96.

—— (1964). *Essays on Ego Psychology.* New York: Int. Univ. Press.

Heimann, P. (1950). On counter-transference. *Int. J. Psychoanal.* 31: 81–84.

Isakower, O. (1965). Comment in seminar.

Jabobs, T. (1993). Discussion at meetings of the International Psychoanalytic Association, Amsterdam.

Jacobson, J. (1994). Signal affects and our psychoanalytic confusion of tongues. *J. Amer. Psychoanal. Assn.* 42: 15–42.

Kaplan, D. (1990). Personal communication.

Katan, A. (1961). Some thoughts about the role of verbalization in early childhood. *Psychoanal. Study Child* 16: 184–188.

Kernberg, O. (1975). *Borderline Conditions and Pathological Narcissism.* New York: Aronson.

—— (1976). *Object Relations Theory and Clinical Psychoanalysis.* New York: Aronson.

Killingmo, B. (1985a). Problems in contemporary psychoanalytic theory. I. Controversial issues. *Scand. J. Psychol.* 26: 53–62.

—— (1985b). Problems in contemporary psychoanalytic theory. II. Lines of advance. *Scand. J. Psychol.* 26: 63–72.

—— (1989). Conflict and deficit: Implications for technique. *Int. J. Psychoanal.* 70: 65–79.

Kohut, H. (1971). *The Analysis of the Self.* New York: Int. Univ. Press.

—— (1977). *The Restoration of the Self.* New York: Int. Univ. Press.

—— (1984). *How Does Analysis Cure?* Chicago: Univ. of Chicago Press.

Kris, E. (1956). The recovery of childhood memories in psychoanalysis. *Psychoanal. Study Child* 11: 54–88.

Lidz, T. (1968). *The Person.* New York: Basic Books.

Lipton, S. (1977). The advantages of Freud's technique as shown in his analysis of the Rat Man. *Int. J. Psychoanal.* 58: 255–273.

Loewald, H. W. (1960). On the therapeutic action of psychoanalysis. *Int. J. Psychoanal.* 41: 16–33.

Mahler, M. S. (1942). Pseudoimbecility: A magic cap of invincibility. *Psychoanal. Q.* 11: 149–164.

—— (1966). Notes on the development of basic moods: The depressive affect. In *Psychoanalysis: A General Psychology,* ed. R. M. Loewenstein, L. M. Newman, M. Schur, and A. J. Solnit. New York: Int. Univ. Press, 152–168.

—— (1972). On the first three subphases of the separation-individuation process. *Int. J. Psychoanal.* 53: 333–338.

Mahler, M. S., Pine, F., and Bergman, A. (1975). *The Psychological Birth of the Human Infant.* New York: Basic Books.

McDevitt, J. B. (1975). Separation-individuation and object constancy. *J. Amer. Psychoanal. Assn.* 23: 713–742.

Meehl, P. (1994). Subjectivity in psychoanalytic inference: The nagging persistence of Wilhelm Fleiss's Achensee question. *Psychoanal. Contemp. Thought* 17: 3–82.

Modell, A. (1984). *Psychoanalysis in a New Context.* New York: Int. Univ. Press.

—— (1994). Common ground or divided ground? *Psychoanal. Inquiry* 14: 201–211.

Ogden, T. (1996). Reconsidering three aspects of psychoanalytic technique. *Int. J. Psychoanal.* 77: 883–899.

Panel (1994). K. R. Eissler's (1953) "The effect of the structure of the ego on psychoanalytic technique." Reported by Kevin Kelly. *J. Amer. Psychoanal. Assn.* 42: 875–882.

Piaget, J. (1937). *The Construction of Reality in the Child.* New York: Basic Books, 1954.

—— (1952). *The Origins of Intelligence in Children.* New York: Int. Univ. Press.

Pine, F. (1976). On therapeutic change: Perspectives from a parent-child model. *Psychoanal. Contemp. Science* 5: 537–569.

—— (1981). In the beginning: Contributions to a psychoanalytic developmental psychology. *Int. Rev. Psychoanal.* 8: 15–33.

—— (1982). The experience of self: Aspects of its formation, expansion, and vulnerability. *Psychoanal. Study Child* 37: 143–167.

—— (1984). The interpretive moment. *Bull. Menninger Clinic* 48: 54–71.

—— (1985). *Developmental Theory and Clinical Process.* New Haven: Yale Univ. Press.

—— (1988). The four psychologies of psychoanalysis and their place in clinical work. *J. Amer. Psychoanal. Assn.* 36: 571–596.

—— (1990). *Drive, Ego, Object, and Self: A Synthesis for Clinical Work.* New York: Basic Books.

—— (1992). From technique to a theory of psychic change. *Int. J. Psychoanal.* 73: 251–254.

—— (1994a). Discussion of "Psychotherapy research and its implications for a theory of therapeutic change" (R. W. Wallerstein). New York Psychoanalytic Society, April 1994.

—— (1994b). Multiple models, clinical practice, and psychoanalytic theory: Response to discussants. *Psychoanal. Inquiry* 14: 212–234.

—— (1996). Commentary. In *The British Schools of Psychoanalysis*, ed. D. Hill and C. Grand. Northvale, N.J.: Aronson, 73–90.

Provence, S., and Lipton, R. (1962). *Infants in Institutions.* New York: Int. Univ. Press.

Psychoanalytic Quarterly (1990). The psychoanalytic process. Ed. S. M. Abend. 59: 527–765.

Rangell, L. (1983). The enduring armature of psychoanalytic theory and method. In *The Human Core. Vol. 2.* Madison, CT: Int. Univ. Press, 1990, 847–862.

Reich, A. (1951). On countertransference. *Int. J. Psychoanal.* 32: 25–31.

Reich, W. (1949). *Character Analysis.* New York: Orgone Institute Press.

Renik, O. (1995). The ideal of the anonymous analyst and the problem of self disclosure. *Psychoanal. Q.* 64: 466–495.

Rockland, L. H. (1989). *Supportive Therapy: A Psychodynamic Approach.* New York: Basic Books.

Sandler, J. (1981). Unconscious wishes and human relationships. *Contemp. Psychoanal.* 17: 180–196.

—— (1988). Psychoanalytic technique and "analysis terminable and interminable." *Int. J. Psychoanal.* 69: 335–345.

Sandler, J., and Rosenblatt, B. (1962). The concept of the representational world. *Psychoanal. Study Child* 17: 128–145.

Schafer, R. (1983). *The Analytic Attitude.* New York: Basic Books.

Seabrook, J. (1996). Feel no pain. *The New Yorker.* July 22, 32–38.

Spitz, R. A. (1957). *No and Yes.* New York: Int. Univ. Press.

—— (1959). *A Genetic Field Theory of Ego Formation.* New York: Int. Univ. Press.

—— (1965). *The First Year of Life.* New York: Int. Univ. Press.

Stone, J., and Church, J. (1973). *Childhood and Adolescence.* New York: Random House.

Stone, L. (1954). The widening scope of indications for psychoanalysis. *J. Amer. Psychoanal. Assn.* 2: 567–594.

—— (1961). *The Psychoanalytic Situation.* New York: Int. Univ. Press.

Strachey, J. (1934). The nature of the therapeutic action of psychoanalysis. *Int. J. Psychoanal.* 15: 127–159.

Sullivan, H. S. (1953). *The Interpersonal Theory of Psychiatry.* New York: Norton.

Waelder, R. (1936). The principle of multiple function. *Psychoanal. Q.* 5: 45–62.

—— (date unknown). Talk to the New York Psychoanalytic Society.

Wallerstein, R. S. (1985). *Forty Two Lives in Treatment: A Study of Psychoanalysis and Psychotherapy.* New York: Guilford.

——. (1988). One psychoanalysis or many? *Int. J. Psychoanal.* 69: 5–21.

—— (1994). Psychotherapy research and its implications for a theory of therapeutic change: Forty year overview. New York Psychoanalytic Society, April 1994.

Werman, D. (1984). *The Practice of Supportive Psychotherapy.* New York: Brunner Mazel.

Winnicott, D. W. (1960). Ego distortion in terms of true and false self. In *The Maturational Processes and the Facilitating Environment.* New York: Int. Univ. Press, 1965, 37–55.

—— (1963a). Psychiatric disorders in terms of infantile maturational processes. In *The Maturational Processes and the Facilitating Environment.* New York: Int. Univ. Press, 1965, 230–241.

—— (1963b). The development of the capacity for concern. In *The Maturational Processes and the Facilitating Environment.* New York: Int. Univ. Press, 1965, 73–82.

—— (1963c). From dependence towards independence in the development of the individual. In *The Maturational Processes and the Facilitating Environment.* New York: Int. Univ. Press, 1965, 83–92.

—— (1965). *The Maturational Processes and the Facilitating Environment.* New York: Int. Univ. Press.

—— (1971). The use of an object and relating through identifications. In *Playing and Reality.* New York: Basic Books, 86–94.

Youngerman, J. (1979). The syntax of silence: Electively mute therapy. *Int. Rev. Psychoanal.* 6: 283–295.

Index